dilli ki shaan

dilli ki shaan

Discover Delhi

THE HERITAGE OF INDIA'S CAPITAL CITY

talking CUB
An imprint of Speaking Tiger Books

INTACH
Indian National Trust for Art and Cultural Heritage

Heritage Education and Communication Service (HECS)

Talking Cub
Speaking Tiger Books LLP
4381/4 Ansari Road, Daryaganj, New Delhi–110002, India

Heritage Education and Communication Service (HECS)
Indian National Trust for Art and Cultural Heritage (INTACH)
71, Lodhi Estate, New Delhi -110003
Tel: 24631818, 24637172, 24632267, 24632269; Fax: 91-11-24611290
Email: hecsintach@gmail.com, intachhecs@gmail.com
Website: www.intach.org, www.youngintach.org

This edition published in Talking Cub, an imprint of Speaking Tiger Books, in association with INTACH in paperback in 2020

ISBN: 978-93-82343-33-2
eISBN: 978-93-89958-66-9

Concept and Text Development
Purnima Datt
Shivaa Rawat

Content Research
Sanjana Anand

Content Writing and Editing
Sanjana Anand
Sanjoli Mathur
Shivaa Rawat

Illustrations
Ashmi Nayar
Geetika Gunjan
Ira Nagar

Acknowledgements
Dr. Swapna Liddle
INTACH Delhi Chapter
INTACH Natural Heritage Division

Design and Layout: Arrt Creations
Printed by: Pragati Pinters, Naraina, New Delhi-28

CONTENTS

FOREWORD

I extend my heartiest congratulations to the Heritage Education and Communication Service (HECS) for compiling a handbook on Delhi's unique natural, cultural and living heritage.

The Heritage Education and Communication Service (HECS) was set up in 1998 and has completed 20 years. It runs a network of around 3,900 heritage clubs, trains teachers and works on campaigns and activities with schools, as well as, colleges across the country.

HECS creates heritage awareness among the youth and runs heritage clubs with the support of its over 200 chapters spread across the country. It produces a variety of resource material and publications for schools and colleges. These are used as a part of the training for teachers too. HECS's initiative of spreading INTACH's vision is further disseminated through the Young INTACH Newsletters on quarterly basis for its heritage clubs. In a fun and at the same time highly educational way, it strives to make heritage learning interesting as well as memorable.

This latest publication *Dilli ki Shaan* – Discover Delhi explores Delhi's heritage. It highlights the rich natural, built and living heritage of the city. It offers information on the flora and fauna of Delhi. It also discusses the many cities of Delhi, the plethora of monuments and the different arts, cultural traditions and cuisines.

I would congratulate Ms Purnima Datt, Principal Director, HECS and her team for carrying forward INTACH's mission of heritage awareness with much enthusiasm and dedication.

I wish them the very best in all their endeavours.

Maj. Gen. (Retd.) L.K. Gupta
Chairman
Indian National Trust for Art and Cultural Heritage (INTACH)

July 2020

INTRODUCTION

Many of us think we are quite familiar with the heritage of Delhi. We know about the 'seven cities', we know of its three UNESCO World Heritage Sites and many other monuments. But there is much more to heritage than just important monuments. Old courtyard homes (havelis), or historic neighbourhoods, where people still live, such as Shahjahanabad and Mehrauli, are also heritage. It is also wrong to think that heritage has to be hundreds of years old. Some important buildings constructed just a few decades ago are heritage of the future, and we must protect them. It is also not true that heritage only consists of buildings. Crafts, arts, literature, customs, festivals, and even food, are part of a 'living' heritage. The natural landscape is also an important part of our heritage, shaped by natural forces as well as human interventions over hundreds of years.

This book tells us about the many different aspects of Delhi's heritage, and their relevance to our lives. It is also interactive, with many suggestions for fun activities and projects. Its photographs and illustrations make it a pleasure to read.

Dr Swapna Liddle
Convenor
INTACH Delhi Chapter

July 2020

Delhi: Through the Ages

An Introduction

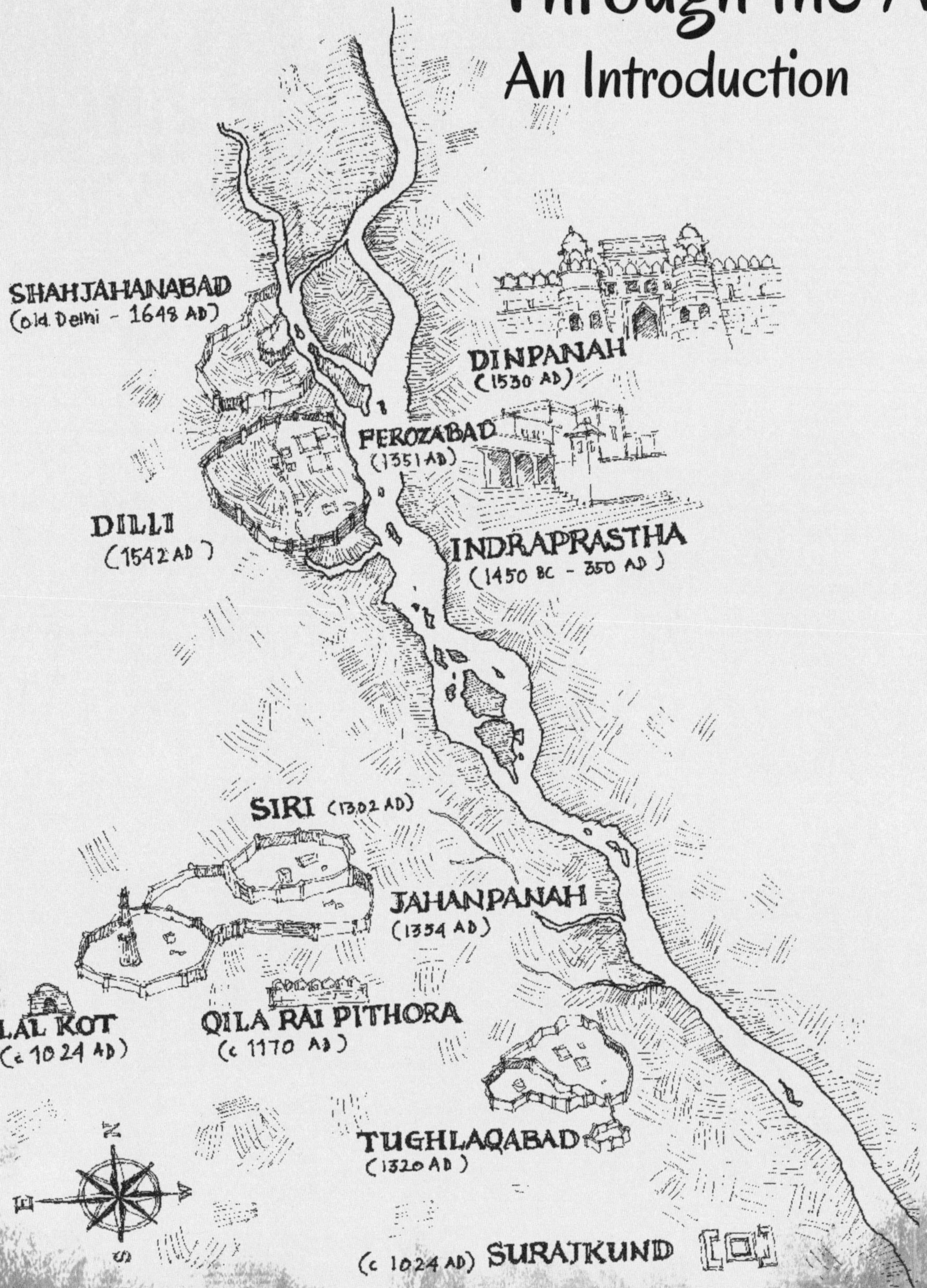

DELHI: THROUGH THE AGES

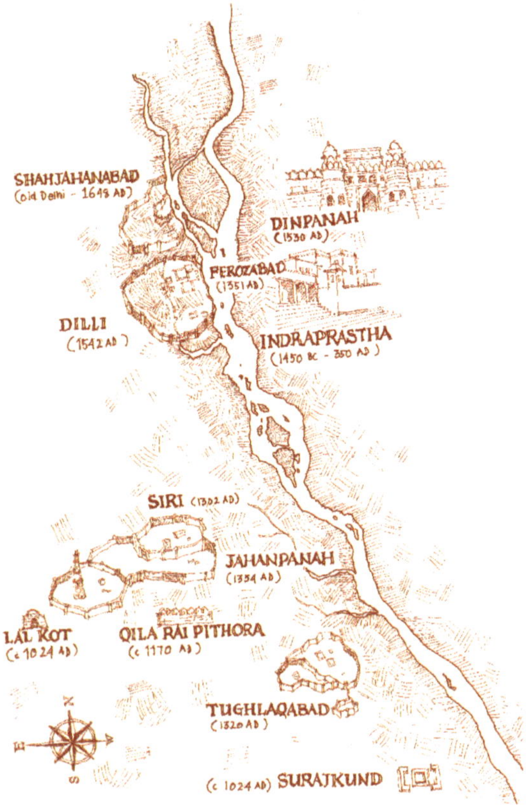

"Here we stand in Delhi City, symbol of old India and the new. It is not the narrow lanes and houses of Old Delhi or the wide spaces and rather pretentious buildings of New Delhi that count, but the spirit of this ancient city. For Delhi has been an epitome of India's history with its succession of glory and disaster, and with its great capacity to absorb many cultures and yet remain itself. It is a gem with many facets, some bright and some darkened by age, presenting the course of India's life and thought during the ages. Even the stones here whisper to our ears of the ages of long ago and the air we breathe is full of the dust and fragrance of the past, as also of the fresh and piercing winds of the present."

Jawaharlal Nehru, Extract from *Towards a New Equilibrium*,
Convocation Address, University of Delhi, 6th December 1958

Delhi is among the oldest Indian cities with numerous years of history and culture. Its history with human settlements can be traced as far back as the Palaeolithic period. A prehistoric site in Delhi region has been excavated at Anangpur village. Close by, remnants of palaeo-channels (ancient courses) of the Yamuna have also been identified.

Delhi has been the capital of several different empires over the centuries and is said to have been founded by the Tomar Rajput rulers. The historic cities of Delhi are Lal Kot, Qila Rai Pithora, Siri, Tughlaqabad, Jahanpanah, Firozabad, and Dinpanah; with the cities of Shahjahanabad and Lutyen's New Delhi identifiable even today.

Strategically situated between the Ridge and the shifting course of the Yamuna river, Delhi has been an important political centre for many empires. It was the central point for trade routes in the northern plains. In 1911, Britain shifted the capital from Calcutta to Delhi, and after Independence, in 1947, it became the national capital of India. It was chosen as the capital because of its geographical position.

Tughlaqabad Fort

DILLI KI KAHAANI

According to myths and legends, Indraprastha was perhaps the first city of Delhi. It was built by Maya, the architect for the Pandavas around 5,000 years ago. The Mahabharata describes the palace built by the Pandavas as "furnished with golden walls, archways, and adorned with many varied pictures" (Mahabharata, Sabha Parva 2).

A number of myths are associated with the origin of the name 'Delhi'. According to Persian historian Feristah and the First Surveyor General of the Archaeological Survey of India (ASI), Sir Alexander Cunningham, Delhi received its name from King Dhilu who ruled during the Mauryan period and was overthrown by the Scynthians.

MYTHICAL PALACE

Imagine you are a Pandava King, draw and describe the palace you would be living in.

Purana Qila

DELHI QUOTES

- *Killi to dhilli bhai, Tomar bhaya to mat hin*
  The pillar has become loose, and thus the Tomar shall lose his kingdom).
  This is the story of the downfall of the Tomar dynasty, from where Delhi is said to have derived its name.
- *Dilli Dur Ast*
  (Delhi is far away)
  King Ghiyas-ud-din Tughlaq was cursed by Sufi Saint Nizamuddin Auliya. The Sufi saint said to the king, "Hunuz Dilli dur ast", meaning Delhi is still far away for you. And the king died before entering Delhi. So, the prophecy!
- *Kaun jaaye 'Zauq' par, Dilli ki galiyan chhod kar*
  (But who wants to leave the streets of Delhi?)
  Mohammed Ibrahim Zauq, a well-known Urdu poet of the Mughal court refused to leave Delhi in the 19th century and continued to write amidst political turmoil.

Find out the background and stories associated with interesting quotes about Delhi.

MY CITY AND I

Few cities of the world can parallel the long and historic status of Delhi.

Come, let us explore Delhi with some activities…

DELHI DIARY

- What is your name? Where do you reside in Delhi?
- How long have you and your family lived in Delhi? Talk to your grandparents about their oldest memories of the city. Pen down interesting stories or memories.
- Are there any interesting landmarks or stories associated with the area you reside in?
- Which historic landmarks have you visited in Delhi? Which is your favorite? Imagine you are writing to your pen-friend about your city. What will you tell your friend?

  Hint: Describe the landmarks, myths and legends.
- Choose an image that symbolises the city for you, something personal that you associate with Delhi and give reasons for your selection.
- Do a similar activity for your own city. What does the city mean to you?

Tomb of Mohammad Shah Sayyid

Natural Heritage

YAMUNA – DELHI'S LIFELINE

Originating in the Yamunotri glacier in the Himalayas, the Yamuna flows through the Lesser Himalayas and the Shivalik Ranges and then descends into the Doon Valley. Passing through the revered pilgrimage site of Paonta Sahib, it reaches Tajewala in Haryana. The river then enters Delhi, having travelled around 400 km from its point of origin. The Yamuna travels across the five states of Uttarakhand, Himachal Pradesh, Haryana, Uttar Pradesh and Delhi before joining the Ganga at Allahabad. It is the second largest tributary of the Ganga.

Yamuna in History

The Yamuna has played an important role in influencing the history of Delhi. Most ancient cities of Delhi were built on its banks. Indraprastha (city of the Pandavas) is believed to have existed on the banks of the Yamuna. During the reign of Feroz Shah Tughlaq, the city of Ferozabad was also built on the banks of the Yamuna. Later, Mughal Emperor Humayun built his capital Dinpanah near this river. The Imperial capital of Emperor Shahjahan – Shahjahanabad on its banks was another example of the importance that this river held.

Yamuna Stories

According to legends, the Yamuna is the Daughter of the Sun God and sister of Yama – the God of Death. According to the Rig Veda, Yama and Yami were the first mortal twins born to Surya, the Sun God, and were said to be the first man and woman on the earth. The Yamuna is worshipped as a Goddess for she waters the seeds that are brought to life with the help of the sun and warmth provided by her father, the Sun God.

It is said that the Yamuna was brought to earth by the penance of the Seven Sages (Kashyapa, Vashishta, Gautama, Jamadagni, Vishwamitra, Bhardwaja and Atri) for millions of years in ancient times after which she descended on a mountain called Kalinda. She is therefore also called Kalindi.

The river is a symbol of divine love as Lord Krishna is said to be present in the stones of Govardhan and the soil of Vrindavan while his beloved is present in the Yamuna. He is the mountain and his beloved is the river!

Poet Kalidasa in the Gupta Period described the confluence of the 'white waters' of the Ganga with the 'blue waters' of the Yamuna.

DID YOU KNOW?

The Nigambodh on the banks of the Yamuna is among the oldest cremation ghats in Delhi. Here, Lord Brahma bathed and recovered his lost memory of sacred books (Vedas) and hence it acquired the name Nigambodh (literally meaning realization of knowledge).

YAMUNA YATRA

Take a journey down the Yamuna by reading excerpts from a diary written by a young heritage lover. Read her experiences and examine the condition of the river.

DESTINATION: Yamunotri, Uttarakhand (source of the Yamuna)

Dear Diary,
I saw the magnificent shimmering Yamuna glacier at an altitude of 10,804 feet! It distressed me to see people scatter polythene bags everywhere... After a few miles, the solid icy river degenerated into a brownish, slushy composition which is evidence of the harmful side effects of global warming... By cleaning the immediate area of as much non-biodegradable waste as possible, I felt as if, I had done my bit.

DESTINATION: Delhi

Dear Diary,
The river was inert, lacking aquatic life. The stench of decay was repulsive...
It was painful to see the emerald green river reduced to black sludge with tonnes of litter. What can I do here?

Resourceful River

A river supports people in many ways.

- Drinking water
- Irrigation
- Fertile soil
- Aquatic life
- Ground water recharge
- Transport
- Hydel energy
- Recreation

RIVER AT RISK

With high levels of pollution in the Yamuna, which of these function still apply today?
Do these functions harm the river?
Have a debate on this topic.

PAANI PANCHAYAT

Hold a mock panchayat representing four groups interested in the Yamuna. These could include industrialists, farmers, environmentalists, residents or the local welfare association. Address the problems, solutions, and possible strategies for each group.

Questions to ask:

- People's knowledge about the Yamuna.
- People's opinions/feelings towards the Yamuna.
- Awareness about the benefits of the Yamuna.
- Willingness to help change the condition of the Yamuna.

Form a group dedicated to cleaning the river:

- Plan how the group can help. They can spread awareness and extend their outreach.
- Maintain a record of an action plan, its execution and any challenges faced.

YAMUNA TODAY

Once the lifeline which nurtured many civilizations and cities on its banks, the Yamuna today is in a deplorable state. It suffers from inadequate flow and an extremely high level of pollution. According to the Central Pollution Control Board (CPCB), the water quality of the Yamuna falls under the category 'E' which makes it fit only for recreation and industrial cooling, completely ruling out possibility for aquatic life. The pollution of the Yamuna from domestic and industrial discharges from Delhi, Ghaziabad, Noida, Faridabad, Mathura and Agra has rendered it unfit for consumption.

Rapid urbanization, industrial effluents, domestic waste water, pollution from agriculture, solid wastes, garbage, encroachments on the river banks, backlog in sanitation, and waste water management have indeed contributed to its deteriorating state.

Damn the Drains!

A major source of pollution (to the extent of about 80%) is the discharge from drains.

There are 22 major drains that discharge treated and untreated waste water into the Yamuna. These include -

1. Najafgarh drain
2. Magazine Road drain
3. Khyber Pass drain
4. Metcalfe House drain
5. Qudsia Bagh drain
6. Mori Gate drain

CLEAN THE DRAIN

- Find out names of other drains.
- What can be done to check the water flow from these drains?
- Can the water be treated at the source and not allowed to enter the Yamuna?

RIVER RESEARCH

What could be done to rejuvenate the Yamuna?

Prepare an action plan and send to the Jal Board.

Suggested measures to rejuvenate the Yamuna

- Proper Management and Treatment of Wastewater
  - Conserve water and use it effectively
  - Promote waste water treatment technologies
  - Manage drainage water efficiently
  - Recycle and re-use waste water
  - Finance waste water management schemes
  - Upgrade sewage treatment plants
- Strategy for the Yamuna river bed conservation and development
- Sewage disposal
- Solid Waste Management and setting up public toilets
- Legislation and fines
- Raising awareness
- Creation of regulated flood plain reservoirs for storing excess monsoon overflow at suitable locations

RUGGED RIDGE

"The five biggest favours bestowed by trees are like five Mahayagyas.
They give fuel to the families, shade and resting place to the travellers, nests to the birds,
and medicines from their leaves, roots and bark."

Varaha Purana 162: 41–42

The natural forest cover of Delhi is a thorn forest. It is a semi-arid environment and the most common trees found in the thorn forests are acacias.

The best example of Delhi's forest is the Ridge or the Aravalli. Delhi's Ridge is the northern extension of the ancient Aravalli range. It is the oldest fold mountain in India which is 2.5 billion years old. The range rose in a Precambrian event called the Aravalli Delhi orogen. In the geological past, the Aravalli must have been of a greater height but has been worn down by millions of years of weathering and erosion.

The Aravalli hills extend erratically within Delhi and can be categorized under four zones:

- *Old Delhi or Northern Ridge* near Delhi University – This comprises the smallest part of the urban forest, covering less than a hundred hectares.
- *New Delhi or Central Ridge* from Sadar Bazar to Dhaula Kaun – This area is spread over more than eight hundred hectares and is the only wooded area with surviving native trees.
- *Mehrauli or South-Central Ridge* near Jawahar Lal Nehru University – Spread over six hundred hectares, the area used to be a quarry site which degraded the soil cover of the region thereby, affecting the vegetation as well.
- *Tughlakabad or Southern Ridge* (including, the Asola and Bhatti wildlife sanctuaries) – This is the largest forest region, covering more than six thousand hectares. The artificial water bodies present here have made it suitable for migratory water birds.

One can find trees, like the Hingot, the Khair and the Dhak on the Ridge that are not found anywhere else in Delhi. The Ridge is the 'green lung' of Delhi, 'pollution controller', 'climate moderator' and 'groundwater recharger'. It prevents soil erosion besides being a wildlife habitat. It is interesting to note that this 'green lung' of Delhi was not completely a 'gift of nature', rather a lot of the present vegetation was planted. These planted species were not indigenous to the Ridge.

EXPLORING THE RIDGE

- Take a walk through the Ridge. Identify some of the trees and collect specimens of leaves and flowers. Make a scrapbook. NOTE: Do not pluck anything, just collect those fallen on the ground.
- Write about your trip to the Ridge. Mention the sound, feel, smell of the forest, as well as, any plastic or soil pollutants you may notice.
- Make a poster on 'Saving the Ridge'.

DID YOU KNOW?

Article 51 of the Indian Constitution states that it is the fundamental duty of Indian citizens to protect and improve the natural environment which includes forests, lakes, rivers, and so on...

PROTECTING THE RIDGE

The 19th century saw loss of patches of the Ridge, as new areas like Paharganj and Paharipur were created. Post Independence, rapid urbanization and increasing population growth depleted the Ridge.

Medieval Period

During the Medieval period, the first four cities of Delhi were located on the Ridge, as the hills provided a natural line of defence. In the 14th century, Feroz Shah Tughlaq fenced off an area of the Ridge where he planted several trees to improve the hunting potential of the region. It is part of the Northern Ridge today.

British Period

When Delhi became the capital in 1912, the British began paying attention to the afforestation of the Ridge to serve as a backdrop for their new city. According to Municipal records, as many as; 3,000 indigenous trees were planted. Neem and Babool were planted between 1878 and 1879. In 1913, the British rulers decided to preserve the Central Ridge by protecting it under Section 4 of Act VII of the Indian Forest Act, 1878.

Post Independence

After India's Independence in 1947, Delhi's population expanded rapidly. As a result, the pressure on its natural resources increased. However, with the establishment of the Forest Wing in 1950, the administration had taken up the planned work of managing the Ridge through the norms of forestry. The M.C. Mehta case resulted in the setting-up of the Ridge Management Board (on 6 October 1995) under the Chairmanship of the Chief Secretary with the Head of the Forest Department of the Delhi Government as its Member Secretary.

Ridge and The Revolt of 1857

During the Revolt of 1857, the British troops were stationed in the northern part of the Ridge, to take advantage of its height.

PROTECT THE RIDGE

The Ridge is gradually disappearing. We must do something to protect this natural heritage! Research on the deforestation of the Ridge today.

Guiding questions:

- What are the main causes of deforestation in the region?
- What are the consequences of deforestation – for people, for animals and for the environment?
- Who benefits from deforestation?
- Are trees being replaced and replanted? Are all these trees indigenous to Delhi?
- What are the governments, NGOs, environmentalists doing to protect the Ridge?
- What can you do to protect the Ridge?

TREASURED TREES

Delhi's native trees are typically short, thorny and adapted to the dry climate of Delhi. Some of these are found in the Ridge. Today, most trees found in Delhi are exotic. These are found lining streets, in parks and gardens, replacing the original native flora and beautifying the landscape.

TREE MYTHS

Find out more about the trees of Delhi. Write about the myths, legends and interesting stories associated with them.

Some Trees of Delhi

Babool

BOTANICAL NAME – *Acacia nilotica*
COMMON ENGLISH NAME – *Egyptian Mimosa*
LOCAL NAME – *Keekar, Desi Babool*

Description – A middle-sized thorny tree with a blackish bark. It has bright yellow 'pom-pom' like, flowers clustered together.

Distribution – Connaught Place was built on a Babool forest which was later cleared. Now this tree can be found in the Hauz Khas District Park and in the Jaunpur ravines.

Siris

BOTANICAL NAME – *Albizia lebbeck*
COMMON ENGLISH NAME – *East Indian Walnut*
LOCAL NAME – *Sirish, Siras*

Description – A middle-sized deciduous tree, in the newer areas of Delhi. It is distinguished by its fragrant long greenish-yellow stamens with 'powder-puff' like flowers.

Distribution – It can be found in Moti Bagh, Jawaharlal Nehru University (JNU) campus, parks and gardens.

Amaltas

BOTANICAL NAME – *Cassia fistula*
COMMON ENGLISH NAME – *Indian Laburnum*
LOCAL NAME – *Girmala, Rajbrikh*

Description – A middle-sized deciduous tree with beautiful bright yellow flowers which shed in April or May. It has feather compound leaves. The fruits are found in long pipes, which are initially green and later, turn black.

Distribution – Amrita Shergil Marg and Akbar Road are lined with Amaltas. It is often found in parks and gardens as well.

Khair

BOTANICAL NAME – *Acacia catechu*
COMMON ENGLISH NAME – *Black Cutch Tree*
LOCAL NAME – *Khair Babool*

Description – A thorny deciduous tree, the Khair is a native tree of Delhi. It has adapted to the harsh Delhi weather. The Khair has twice feathered compound leaves with clustered white flowers.

Distribution – It is now scattered over the Central and Southern Ridge.

PLANT A TREE

- Select a tree (try to select an indigeneous species).
- Make sure your selected tree can adapt to extreme climatic variations, ranging from near droughts to chilling winters.
- Dig a hole large enough so that we can completely cover the roots of the plant. The soil should be moist and compost should be mixed.
- Lightly press the soil around the planted tree.
- Be careful of where you plant the tree. You do not want it to grow near cables or building foundations.
- Water the seedlings regularly, especially, during summer.
- Remember, trees need love! Return to the site in weeks and months after you have planted your seedling to carry out any necessary maintenance.

WHAT CAN I PLANT?

- Amaltas
- Dhau
- Neem
- Palash
- Roheda
- Siris

Vilaiti Keekar

BOTANICAL NAME – *Prosopis juliflora*

COMMON ENGLISH NAME – *Mesquite*

LOCAL NAME – *Angrezi Keekar*

Description – A medium-sized thorny tree introduced to the Delhi Ridge in 1915 from South America. It bears twice feathered compound leaves with small greenish-yellow flowers.

Distribution – It is, by far, the most dominant tree in the Delhi Ridge and is found almost everywhere in the city.

Dhau

BOTANICAL NAME – *Anogeissus pendula*

COMMON ENGLISH NAME – None

LOCAL NAME – *Dhoy, Dhao*

Description – A short crooked deciduous tree with a silvery trunk. It has small simple leaves with tiny yellowish-green flowers.

Distribution – This tree is native of the Aravalli, though now in danger of dying out.

Neem

BOTANICAL NAME – *Azadirachta indica*

COMMON ENGLISH NAME – *Margosa*

LOCAL NAME – *Neem, Nimb*

Description – A medium semi-ever-green tree with a short trunk and dense canopy. This tree was not native to Delhi but has been naturalised and is known for its medicinal properties.

Distribution – It is a common tree in the Ridge and inside the JNU campus. It is fairly scattered across the city.

Dhak

BOTANICAL NAME – *Butea monosperma*

COMMON ENGLISH NAME – *Flame of the Forest*

LOCAL NAME – *Palash, Tesu*

Description – A medium-sized deciduous tree with pale brown flaky bark. The Dhak is recognised for its bright orange flowers. It is a native Delhi tree that can withstand frost, water-logging and poor soil.

Distribution – It can be found in the Ridge and large gardens, like Nehru Park.

AVENUE TREES OF NEW DELHI

"Trees will be everywhere, in every garden however small it be, and along the sides of every roadway, and Imperial Delhi will be in the main a sea of foliage."

Captain George Swinton, Chairman of the Town-Planning Committee, Preliminary Report, 1912

The British contributed to the greenery of Delhi by planting trees along roadsides or pathways, called avenue plantation. William Mustoe, Director of Horticulture, was responsible for the planting of New Delhi's avenue trees. These avenue trees structure the space, giving it a distinct identity; they act as a sound buffer and arrest air pollution. Most of the mature avenue trees of Delhi are evergreen species.

There are six main avenue trees which have been planted along various roads in the city. These are:

- **Jamun** – Tughlaq Road, Rajaji Tyagraj Marg.
- **Neem** – Safdarjung Road, Lodi Road, Prithviraj Road, Ashoka Road.
- **Arjun** – Janpath.
- **Imli** – Akbar Road.
- **Sausage Tree** – Humayun Road, Amrita Shergill Marg.
- **Baheda** – Barakhamba Road.

Mangarbani

Patches of forests dedicated to deities or ancestral spirits are called sacred groves. The Mangarbani Forest is a sacred forest, in the Aravalli Hills, in the memory of Gudariya Baba, a local holy man. However, these days, this sacred element is sadly not relevant due to a rise in commercialization. The forest trees are being cut down for mining, timber and illegal encroachments. The law is not stringent enough to protect this green patch and environmentalists are afraid that if nothing is done now, the Aravalli forest will disappear.

SENSE–A–TIONAL TREES

We experience the world through five different senses – sight, sound, touch, smell and taste.

- First pick a tree you like.
- Hold one of its leaves upto the light. Look at the shape of the leaf and try to draw it. Does it have ridges or is it smooth?
- Crush the leaf in your hand and smell it. How would you describe the smell? Now lightly put the tip of your tongue on the edge of the crushed leaf. Does it have a taste?
- Close your eyes and touch the bark of the tree let your fingers sense its texture. Is it smooth or rough? Does the bark have a pattern?
- Stand very still and listen. What sounds come from the tree? Are there any birds sounds? Do the leaves make a sound?
- Make a tree notebook and put all your sense-a-tional observation of different trees down. You will be surprised.
- How does the power of your senses help you understand trees?

GRACEFUL GARDENS

A historic garden is defined as an *"architectural and horticultural composition of interest to the public from the historical or artistic point of view. As such, it is to be considered as a monument."*

The Charter on Historic Gardens
(Florence Charter, 1981)

Gardens are an important component of a city's landscape. They are sites of recreation and reflect the cultural expression of the dynasties in power.

Medieval Period

Firoz Shah Tughlaq of the Delhi Sultanate built 1,200 gardens in and around Delhi. The Mughals planted many gardens in Delhi. About six exist today – Jahanara Garden, Qudsia Bagh, Roshanara Bagh, Shalimar Bagh, Beriwala Bagh and Talkatora Garden.

The Mughals introduced the charbagh style to Indian architecture. Charbagh means four gardens. It is a Persian style garden layout based on four Gardens of Paradise mentioned in the Qur'an. In Delhi, the charbagh garden can be seen at the Humayun's Tomb and Safdarjung Tomb.

British Period

Edwin Lutyens pictured New Delhi as a green garden city. Some of the famous gardens designed during the British period were the Lodi Garden and the Mughal Gardens.

Lodi Gardens was called the Bagh-i-Jud or the ground for royal burials in the 15th century. It is famous for its Lodi and Sayyid dynasty tombs. The Lodi Garden, as we know it today, was designed by the British in 1936. Under their reign, it was named as Lady Willingdon Park. It was later renamed Lodi Garden due to its historic and architectural importance.

The Mughal Garden of Rashtrapati Bhavan was also inspired by the Mughal charbagh style as well. Lutyens brought in Mughal style horticulture traditions and the English flower garden style to create this masterpiece.

Marvels of Lodi Garden

According to a joint survey by the New Delhi Municipal Council (NDMC) and the Green Circle, a total of 7,055 trees of 189 species can be found in the Lodi Garden. It is home to one of the tallest tree in Delhi – the Buddha Coconut.

Roses of Rashtrapati Bhavan

Roses are an important part of the Mughal gardens with over 120 varieties. One can find roses named after famous people, like, Mother Teresa, Queen Elizabeth, Abraham Lincoln and Jawaharlal Nehru.

Post Independence

Post Independence, the Municipal Corporation of Delhi (MCD), Central Public Works Department (CPWD) and Delhi Development Authority (DDA) established small community parks and gardens of Delhi, like the Buddha Jayanti Park, Talkatora Gardens and Gulmohar Park.

Named after the former Prime Minister, Jawaharlal Nehru, Nehru Park was established in 1969. The park has a variety of plants, like the Gulmohar, Ashoka, Palm, Neem, Champa and many seasonal flowers. It is now a hub for cultural activities, like Music in the Park, International Jazz Festival.

The Garden of Five Senses located in Mehrauli opened in 2003. The garden is designed to excite our five senses with its natural beauty, giving an enchanting opportunity to see, hear, touch and smell our natural surroundings.

Flower Fusion

- Phoolwalon-Ki- Sair meaning 'procession of the florists' is an annual celebration by the flower sellers of Delhi. It is a three-day festival, held in the month of September and represents Delhi's unity in diversity.
- The three-day Garden Tourism Festival is held annually in the month of February. Around 15,000 plants, including, potted plants, foliage, flowers, and medicinal plants are displayed.

GARDEN OF PEACE

Design a layout for a 'Peace Garden'.

- Discuss which plants to grow with a gardener. The aim is to create something beautiful.
- Once the garden is ready, you must take care of it.

NATURE WALK

Walk in your local park, and then in Lodi Garden or any such garden in your city. Compare the conditions of both these parks.

- Is there a difference?
- If yes, give reasons.

WILD WATCH

The Ridge was full of animals several years back. It was home to animals like, the tiger, leopard, hyena, wolf, jackal and fox. The Gazetteer of Delhi (1883-84), in a note on its fauna, recorded pigs (boars), foxes, hares on the banks of Yamuna. Blackbucks were found almost everywhere. Even until the 1960s, wild boars were seen around the Rashtrapati Bhavan and it was easy to spot deer near Nizamuddin. Unfortunately, as a result of urbanization and expansion, wildlife in the city has considerably diminished.

DID YOU KNOW ?

The National Zoological Park in Delhi is home to 1,350 animals with almost 130 species from around the world.

Leopard

Panthera pardus (Linnaeus, 1758)
ORDER – *Carnivora*
FAMILY – *Felidae*
COMMON ENGLISH NAME – *Leopard and Panther*
HINDI NAME – *Tendua, Chita bagh*

Description – Smaller than a tiger, the leopard is a quick reacting mammal. It has a long body with yellow fur and black rosettes. Leopards can hide themselves on a tree or rocky outcrop and drag a large carcass up the tree.

Distribution – Asola Bhatti Wildlife Sanctuary, Yamuna Biodiversity Park. Leopard and human conflict is a major concern today.

Nilgai

Boselaphus tragocamelus Pall
ORDER – *Cetartiodactyla*
FAMILY – *Bovidae*
COMMON ENGLISH NAME – *Blue Bull*
HINDI NAME – *Nilgau*

Description – It is the largest Asian antelope in India. The nilgai is more horse-like than cow-like. It is interesting to note that it drinks regularly during the hot season but can go two to three days without water in cool weather.

Distribution – JNU campus, Sanjay Van, Qutub Institutional area.

Jackal

Canis aureus Linnaeus, 1758
ORDER – *Carnivora*
FAMILY – *Canidae*
COMMON ENGLISH NAME – *Golden Jackal*
HINDI NAME – *Siyaar*

Description – Closer to the wolf in shape, the jackal is smaller in size and far more, adaptable and cunning. The jackal's howling in the night is an indication of its presence. It generally kills small animals.

Distribution – Delhi Ridge and the Asola Bhatti Wildlife.

Common Monkey

Macaca mulatta (Zimmermann, 1780)
ORDER – *Primates*
FAMILY – *Cercopithecidae*
COMMON ENGLISH NAME – *Rhesus Macaque*
HINDI NAME – *Bandar*

Description – Medium-sized, with brown fur and a pink face.

Distribution – North and South Block, Central Secretariat. Delhi faces a huge monkey menace.

Indian Grey Mongoose

Herpestes edwards
ORDER – *Carnivora* FAMILY – *Herpestidae*
COMMON ENGLISH NAME – *Grey Mongoose*
HINDI NAME – *Nevala*

Description – It is a tawny grey furry animal with a pointed face and a bushy tail. This amazing small animal can survive a cobra attack making it one of the most formidable predators of this deadly snake.

Distribution – North Delhi, Ridge Forest, parks and green belts across the city.

MY ANIMAL STORY

Panchatantra, Jataka tales and local folklore often have animal characters with distinct characteristics. Share any one such story, bringing out the animal personality, as well as, the moral of the story.

SANCTUARIES OF DELHI

1. Aravalli Biodiversity Park in the South Central Ridge of Delhi is spread over 692 acres. It is surrounded by the JNU campus, Mehrauli- Mahipalpur road, NH-8, Palam road and Southern Vasant Vihar.
2. Asola Bhatti Wildlife Sanctuary in South Delhi is home to a rich range of birds, as well as, reptiles, amphibians, and mammals. A Conservation Education Centre established here plays a crucial role in generating environmental and conservation awareness.
3. Okhla Bird Sanctuary near Noida is an important bird sanctuary in India. It is home to around 300 Indian bird species.
4. Sultanpur National Park near Gurgaon is famous for bird watching as it is inhabited by approximately 250 species of birds that migrate from East European countries. Some common birds found here are Gray Francolin, Eurasian Thick Knee, Little Cormorant, Purple Sunbird, Paddy Field Pipit and Common Spoonbill.
5. Sanjay Van is a reserved forest in the South Central Ridge extending from the Qutub Institutional area to the Qutub Minar. Spread over 1,582 acres, it had been notified as a reserved forest in 1994 under the Indian Forest Act 1927.
6. Tughuqabad Biodiversity Park located in the Southern Ridge is spread over an area of 200 acres. It was notified as a Biodiversity Park by the Delhi Development Authority (DDA) on the direction of the High Court of Delhi in 2017.
7. Yamuna Biodiversity Park supports more than 1,500 plant and animal species. The diversity of birds has increased from 37 to 196 since 2002, while reptiles have increased from 3 to 18.

Leopards in the City

Rapid urbanization, deforestation and intensive human activities have rapidly depleted the Aravalli Range. Consequently, the habitats inhabited by the animals, including, Leopards has been impacted. Instances of wild animals venturing into human habitations and causing chaos is common. It is necessary to ensure wildlife flourishes and adequate measures are taken to secure their habitats. Besides, preventing dangerous animal encounters by building corridors enabling safe movement for them.

- Collect newspaper clippings to highlight Leopard Human encounters in the National Capital Region.

MY GREEN DIARY

The sanctuaries of Delhi are ideal for visits. Visit a sanctuary and write about it.

- Make a Green Diary to share your experience with photographs and sketches.
- Identify and name some of the trees, animals, birds and insects found here.
- Make two food-chains with the selected flora and fauna.
- List the objects you notice that do not belong to the sanctuary. They can be plastic bottles, wires and so on.
- In the final pages of your Green Diary, share your creative suggestions to improve the sanctuary.

BEAUTIFUL BIRDS

"I've been watching birds from my window and balcony for many years now and have found its a wonderful way of never having to get bored. Because out there, in the world of birds, something always seems to be happening"

Birds from My Window, Ranjit Lal, 2002

Today, as far as, fauna is concerned, Delhi's true fame lies in its bird life. More than 150 bird species can be spotted in Delhi. Some of the birds found in Delhi are the Rock Pigeon, House Crow, Laughing Dove, Peacock, White-Throated Kingfisher, Shikra, Koel, Bulbul, Purple Sun bird, Green Parakeet and so on.

LET US SAVE OUR BIRDS

Find out about birds struggling to survive in your city. Share your suggestions and ideas about ways to save them. For example, if you are involved in bird conservation, please do tell us …

- Feed a bird
- Put water for drinking
- Do not disturb a bird nest
- Do not touch the eggs

Unique Visitors

Delhi is often the destination for many migratory birds like the Painted Stork, Golden Oriole, Rosy Starling, Asian Brown Flycatcher, Crimson Backed Sunbird, and Asian Paradise Flycatcher. We can see these migratory birds in the Okhla Bird Sanctuary, Sultanpur National Park, Dadri Wetlands and they have chosen to visit the Najafgarh nullah and jheel too!

Sacred Birds

Crow: Identified with departed souls or ancestors, the Crow occupies a special place in Hindu rituals of ancestral worship.

Parakeet: Sacred to goddess Meenakshi the Parakeet is shown on her right hand.

Peacock: The Peacock is a vehicle of Lord Kartikeya. In Buddhism, the Jataka stories narrate how Buddha was a golden peacock in a previous birth.

Kite: The Kite is associated with Garuda who is revered as a controller of snakes.

Owl: The Owl is considered to be the vehicle of Goddess Lakshmi and Goddess Chamunda (a form of Durga).

Some Common Birds of Delhi

Rufous Treepie

Dendrocitta vagabunda Latham
HINDI NAME – *Mahalat, Mata*

Description – Treepie is a light brown bird with a black head, a black-tipped gray tail and grayish white wing patches.

Distribution – These birds are found in the Asola Bhatti Sanctuary and around the Indian Institute of Technology.

Blue Rock Pigeon

Columba livia Gmelin
HINDI NAME – *Kabutar*

Description – A common slate-gray bird with glistening metallic-purple, green and magenta sheen on the neck and upper breast, as well as, two dark bars on the wings and across the end of its tail. Its call of 'gootr-goo' is familiar to all!

Distribution – This is our true urban bird which can lay its eggs in nooks of homes.

Commom Pariah Kite

Milvus Migrans Boddaert
HINDI NAME – *Cheel*

Description – Scavengers of the sky, the Pariah Kite or the Black Kite appears black but is actually brown in colour and is distinguished by its forked tail. They can fly at great heights and yet avoid collision.

Distribution – They are found across the city, especially, in large numbers near landfill sites.

Indian Myna

Acridotheres tristis Linnaeus
HINDI NAME – *Desi myna*

Description – This is a familiar bird which is a dark brown colour with a bright yellow beak, legs and yellow patch around its eyes. Other Mynas are Pied Myna, Bank Myna and Brahminy Myna.

Distribution –These birds are found widely across the region.

Rose-Ringed Parakeet

Psittacula krameri
HINDI NAME – *Tota*

Description – Has a grass-green plumage, hooked red bill and a pointed tail. The males have a black and rose-pink collar, which females do not have. They are noisy and are good at mimicking human voices.

Distribution – They can be seen nesting in the Old Fort, Tughlaqabad Fort and Pusa Complex.

Black Drongo

Dicrurus adsimilis Bechstein
HINDI NAME – *Bujanga, Kotwal*

Description – A slender black bird with a unique long, deeply forked tail; these birds are known for being aggresive.

Distribution – The Okhla and Asola Bhatti Wildlife sanctuaries are good places to see these birds up-close.

Common Gray Hornbill

Tockus Birostris Scopoli
HINDI NAME – *Chalotra, Dhanesh*

Description – Medium-sized frugivorous birds with long tails and a long de-curved beak. They make a high pitched sound and are very noisy. They are generally found flying across trees at great heights.

Distribution – These birds are found mainly around the Ridge. They can also be seen in city parks.

House Sparrow

Passer Domesticus Linnaeus
HINDI NAME – *Gauriyya*

Description – Sparrow is the state bird of Delhi. It is a social bird, small in size, grayish-brown in colour with black streaks. Male and female have differences in colour and can be recognized easily.

Distribution – Urban concrete structures and closed glass windows. Electro-magnetic radiation from mobile phone towers has impacted its nesting patterns. Sadly, this little familiar bird has almost disappeared!

COLOURFUL BUTTERFLIES

In a bid to record butterfly species, *Delhi's first ever 'Big Butterfly Count'* was organized by the Conservation Education Centre (Delhi wing of Bombay Natural History Society), the census was a part of the 'butterfly' month which kicked off on 1st September, 2017 at Asola Bhatti Wildlife Sanctuary and aimed at providing an accurate and updated list of butterfly species found across the National Capital Region.

Out of 92 species of butterflies that can be spotted in Delhi, Painted Lady, Indian Fritillary, Indian Red Flash, Common Blue Bottle and Tawny Coaster are rare. The Painted Lady is a large butterfly and its wing span is around 5 to 9 cm. The life span of a Painted Lady Butterfly is 2 to 4 weeks. Indian Fritillary has an orange body and distinctively marked orange wings with black spots. The female has black wing tips. Its body is 27 mm to 38 mm long.

DID YOU KNOW ?

A Butterfly Park opened for public at the Asola Bhatti Wildlife Sanctuary on the occasion of World Environment Day in 2017. An open butterfly conservatory can be found in the Lodi Garden too. Collections of butterflies can be found at the Indian Agricultural Research Institute (IARI). The Bombay Natural History Society (BNHS) with the help of volunteers is establishing butterfly parks/habitats in residential colonies by re-vamping local parks and planting butterfly host plants. Such as, Kareel, Kanthari, Pathar Chatta, Kari Patta, Amaltas and many others.

Species Spotted

Common: Tiny Grass Blue; Plain Tiger; Stripped Tiger; Common Emigrant; Common Grass Yellow; Common Gull.

Rare: Psyche; Red Pierrot; Indian Red Flash; Chocolate Pansy; Dark Clouded Yellow; Pale Palm Dart.

WONDROUS WINGS

- Visit a biodiversity park and try to identify some butterflies.
- Make your own butterfly garden in a pot.
  Useful tips: Plant flowers in groups, as opposed to individuals, in layers and at various heights; use native plants; plant a variety of flowers with different blooming cycles; spread out host plants so as to not attract predators to the groups of eggs or larvae; keep seeds or potted plants readily available in case of plant loss.
- Butterflies are important for the environment and ecology. Find out about the butterfly effect in the context of environment and climate change.
  The Butterfly Effect: It was a concept invented by the the American meteorologist Edward N. Lorenz (1917-2008) to highlight the possibility that small causes may have momentous effects. Initially used in connection with the weather conditions, it has become a metaphor used in diverse contexts today.
- Find out some fun facts about butterflies.
  - *Fun fact:* Butterflies cannot fly if their body temperature is less than 86 degrees.
  - *Fun fact:* The largest butterfly of India is the Southern Birdwing.

Built Heritage

Till 1180 Period of Mauryas, Shungas, and Tomars in Delhi	1180 Prithviraj Chauhan begins his rule
1192 Mohd. Ghor defeats the Rajputs	1192-1290 Power is handed over to the Mamluks; Khiljis take over
1296 Allauddin Khilji takes over from his uncle Jalaluddin	1321 Tughlaqs take over
1398 Timur's invasion leads to the fall of Tughlaqs	1414 Sayyids rule begins under Khizr Khan
1451 Lodis take control	1526 Lodis face defeat at the hands of Babur. A brief period of Surs
1555 Humayun takes over the throne of Delhi	1639 Shahjahan builds the city of Shahjahanabad
1707 Aurangzeb's death; Nadir Shah's invasion; advent of the British	1858 Beginning of British Governance
1911 Delhi is named the capital	1947 India gets Independence with New Delhi as the capital

CITIES OF DELHI

"The city of Delhi is as full of surprises as a good treasure hunt."

Narayani Gupta

(In the foreword to the book *Delhi: Its Monuments and History*, Percival Spear, 1943)

Delhi is often referred to as the 'Rome of Asia' because of its rich heritage and myriad historic monuments ranging from forts and palaces to tombs and historical gardens. Delhi has been the location of at least nine recorded historic cities. Each city has left behind a mark on the landscape of Delhi. Few texts suggest that Raja Dhilu founded the ancient city of Delhi in 800 BCE, but opinions vary.

The first inscriptional mention of Delhi was found on the Bijolia inscription from the Udaipur District of Rajasthan. The inscription talks about the capture of Delhi by the Chauhans.

The cities of Delhi include Lal Kot, Qila Rai Pithora, Mehrauli, Kilugarhi, Siri, Tughlaqabad, Jahanpanah, Firozabad, Khizrbad, Dinpanah, Shahjahanabad and New Delhi.

It is interesting to note that each time a ruler built a fort or palace, a settlement or city quickly grew around it. Yet, these old cities never completely vanished. Several cities that came up across the centuries co-existed with one another.

In the 20th century, the capital city was sprawled across two main cultural precincts – Shahjahanabad and Lutyens' Delhi.

Even today, as we drive through the streets of Delhi, we would come across many monuments, some well-known, others lesser known, hidden behind homes and shining malls, vying for their place in the history of this amazing city.

ANCIENT DELHI

Stone Story

At least three dozen prehistoric sites have been discovered in and around Delhi. For instance, four lower Paleolithic stone tools have been found in the Northern Ridge. The first ever excavation by the Archaeological Survey of India (ASI) was done in 1955 at the Purana Qila. In 1983, an Achelian hand-axe was found in the Jawaharlal Nehru University (JNU) area. Numerous excavations carried out by the ASI at Purana Qila, Mehrauli, Tughlaqabad, Siri Fort, Red Fort, and Salimgarh Fort between 1969 and 2008 have revealed stone artefacts from the ancient empires of the Maurya, Sunga, Saka, Kushan, Gupta, and Post-Gupta. Remains have been found from the Rajput, Sultanate, and Mughal Periods as well.

Artefacts at Purana Qila excavations

AN EXCITING EXCAVATION

Delhi is the city of cities, and excavations here have revealed many artefacts. Find out and write about any one excavation.

Rock Edict Story

In 1966, one of Emperor Asoka's minor rock edicts was discovered near East of Kailash in South Delhi. It is written in Prakrit language and in the Brahmi script. This discovery suggests that even under the Mauryas, Delhi was part of an important region and was at the intersection of trade routes of Northern India.

MY EDICT

Design your own edict and write one rule of good living for today's times in an interesting script of your choice. Explain what each symbol of your script signifies.

Surajkund Story

The city of Surajkund predates the first city of Delhi. One of the most important features here is the Surajkund Tank, believed to have been constructed by the Tomar King, Surajpal. It is said that a Sun Temple existed here. Some ruins of this temple are still visible. Close to the Surajkund Tank is the village of Anangpur, named after the Tomar King, Anangpal. Here, one can still see remains of the wall built by him. Today, Surajkund is the well-known location of the Surajkund Mela which is held in February every year.

PAST vs PRESENT

Write a dialogue between Surajpal of the Tomar Dynasty and a craftsperson who has set up a stall in the Surajkund Mela.

THE CITY OF THE RAJPUTS

MY GREAT ESCAPE

The walls of the ancient cities were reinforced and made very strong to defend them from attacks. Imagine you are a spy who has been discovered by the soldiers of the fort.

Write a story of your escape. Use the following words: tower, moat, high walls, gate, and tank

Capital City in Delhi: Lal Kot, Qila Rai Pithora (Mehrauli Region)
Dynasty: Tomars (Chauhans)
Time Period: 8th-12th century

> *"Water buffaloes might have roamed around the town before the Tomars set up the first historic city; there still are water buffaloes roaming behind the malls and multiplexes and their keepers still live much the same way as their ancestors did."*
>
> Extract from *The Week* 26 June 2011

Towards the end of the first millennium, the Tomar Rajputs came to power around the Aravalli Hills. Towards the 8th century, they expanded their rule over Delhi with its first city at **Lal Kot**, established by Maharaja Anangpal Tomar II. The city of Lal Kot then expanded to what we know today as Qila Rai Pithora, under the Chauhans, in the 12th century.

Monuments

The remains of the Lal Kot walls can still be seen behind the Qutub Complex, adjoining the Mehrauli village and Sanjay Van. Though they are in a ruined state, we can still see that these walls are very strong. They are between 3 to 9 metres thick and in some places they are still 20 metres high. Anangpal II is also said to have built the Anangtal Tank, when this city was founded. Large stonework lined the bottom of the tank, bringing out the engineering genius of this dynasty.

The Iron Pillar in the Qutub Complex is believed to be from the Gupta Period. One theory based on an inscription found on the pillar tells us that it was moved and placed at Lal Kot when the Tomar King, Anangpal II, built his city.

Ruins of the Qila Rai Pithora walls, built under the Chauhans, have also survived due to conservation efforts by ASI. One can still see its remains near the Malviya Nagar Metro Station on Press Enclave Road.

Iron Pillar

THE CITY OF THE SLAVES

CAPITAL CITY IN DELHI: Mehrauli
DYNASTY: Mamluk – Delhi Sultanate
TIME PERIOD: 12th-13th century

In 1192, the Afghan warrior Muhammad of Ghor defeated the Rajputs. After his death in 1206, Qutubud-din Aibak – his slave, declared himself as the Sultan of Delhi – founding the Delhi Sultanate, so called because it had Delhi as its capital. He constructed a number of monuments located in the **Qutub Complex in Mehrauli**, with the most famous being the Qutub Minar.

Monuments

The Qutub Minar is a UNESCO World Heritage Site and the highest stone tower in India 73 metres in height. It is made of red sandstone and marble. The word Qutub means axis or staff. In the 13th century, Qutubud-din Aibak began its construction to announce his victory over the Chauhans. It was built as both a watch tower as well as a victory tower. The architect of this minar was Fazl Ibn Abu'l Maali. It has been described as the most perfect example of a tower known to exist anywhere in the world!

Qutub Minar

Leaning Tower

If you look at the Qutub Minar closely, you will notice that the tower leans a little towards one side. This is because of various earthquakes. Today, ASI looks after the Qutub Minar with great care.

Storey Stories

Qutubud-din Aibak built the first storey. Iltutmish built the second, third, and fourth. In 1369, Firoz Shah Tughlaq added the fifth one. Sikandar Lodi renovated the fifth storey in 1503, which was restored again by the British East India Company in the 1820s.

Lightning Strike

It was struck by lightning multiple times. The first of which was in 1326, and the second in 1368, damaging the top storey, which was reconstructed by Firoz Shah Tughlaq during his rule.

Smith's Folly

In 1803, an earthquake damaged the topmost storey of the Minar. Major Smith replaced it with a cupola with Mughal features. But this received a lot of flak and Governor General Lord Hardinge had it taken down in 1848. Today, it is placed on the outer lawns of the Qutub Complex.

Beautiful Balconies

A unique technique was used to make the balconies. Small arches supporting a series of small brackets together held them up.

HERITAGE WALK

Walk around the Qutub Complex and bring out the most interesting elements of this World Heritage Site.

- Do you think it is well-maintained?
- What suggestions can you come up with, to make this site more tourist-friendly?

MY VICTORY TOWER

Imagine you are the ruler of Delhi. Design your own victory tower and label it to bring out its features.

Iltutmish's Tomb inside the Qutub Complex was built by Iltutmish himself. Constructed using Delhi quartzite and decorated with white marble and red sandstone, it is carved with Arabic inscriptions and Indian designs like the lotus and kalash.

Another important monument here is the Quwwat-ul-Islam Mosque built by Qutubud-din Aibak. It was one of the first mosques of Delhi, built on a raised platform. An interesting fact about this mosque is that it has many temple elements, which have been taken from temples destroyed during the war between the Tomars and Mohammad Ghori's armies. We thus see the pillars adorned with Hindu symbols like kalash and bells. The arch of the screen is made of red sandstone and has inscriptions in Arabic calligraphy.

Alauddin Khilji built two important structures in the Qutub Complex – the Alai Minar and the Alai Darwaza. The Alai Minar was meant to celebrate the victory of Alauddin Khilji in his Deccan campaigns. He wanted the tower to be twice the height of the Qutub Minar. However, with just one storey completed, this tower remained unfinished after the Sultan's death. The Alai Darwaza was thought to be the main gateway to the extension of the Quwwat-ul-Islam Mosque. Finished in red sandstone and marble, the entire gateway is richly covered with geometrical patterns and inscriptions.

Metal Mastery

The Iron Pillar of Chandragupta II is a scientific marvel. It stands near the Qutub Minar in Delhi. The total height of the pillar is 7.2 metres of which 93 cm is underground. The high amount of phosphorus in the iron formed a layer of 'misamite', which has protected the Iron Pillar from rusting. Sir Robert Hadfield's chemical analysis of the Iron Pillar disclosed the following elements – Carbon-0.080%, Silicon-0.046%, Phosphorous-0.114%, Iron-99.720%.

Interesting Inscriptions

The Minar is decorated with verses from the Quran, in beautiful calligraphy. According to the inscriptions on its surface, it was repaired by Firoz Shah Tughlaq (14th century) and Sikandar Lodi (15th century).

THE CITY OF THE KHILJIS

Capital City in Delhi: Siri Fort
Dynasty: Khilji – Delhi Sultanate
Time Period: 13th-14th century

The Khiljis came to power in Delhi in the 13th century. Sultan Alauddin Khilji, considered to be the most powerful ruler of the Delhi Sultanate, built his capital at **Siri** in 1303. The city of Siri was built to defend against the Mongol attacks.

Monuments

The original fort of Siri was oval in shape. Some say that the name Siri comes from the Hindi word 'head'. According to legend, the heads of the defeated Mongol soldiers were displayed on the walls of the fort. But some historians believe that even before the city was founded, there already existed a place called the plain of Siri, where the armies of Alauddin Khilji had fought the Mongol invaders. Inside, Alauddin Khilji built a palace in which stood the Hall of Thousand Pillars. Sadly, nothing of this magnificent hall remains today.

Just beyond the fort walls stand the ruins of the Chor Minar, a tower, claimed to have been used by Alauddin Khilji for punishing thieves and robbers.

Next to the Chor Minar stand the walls of the Idgah Mosque. The inscription dates back to 1404. It records the building of the mosque and the poor and depressing state of the city after the Timurid invasions.

Chor Minar

Alauddin Khilji built a large tank known as Hauz-e-Alai to supply water to the new city. Firoz Shah Tughlaq restored it in the 1350s, and renamed it as Hauz Khas.

WATER WARRIORS

In 2003, INTACH, along with the Delhi Development Authority (DDA) undertook a project to revive the Hauz Khas Lake. It aimed at reusing treated sewage water while encouraging recycling of urban wastewater. As a result of this project, the groundwater in the Hauz Khas village increased.

- Identify a water body which is neglected in your neighbourhood.
- Organize a cleanliness drive around it and devise methods for its regular monitoring.
- Make a poster to spread awareness about cleaning water bodies.

DID YOU KNOW?

Alauddin Khilji constructed the Hall of Thousand Pillars at Siri on the lines of the Thousand Pillar temple at Warangal, in Telangana.

Hauz Khas Complex

THE CITY OF THE TUGHLAQS

DID YOU KNOW?

The Malcha Mahal, hidden inside the Central Ridge was a hunting lodge constructed by Firoz Shah Tughlaq in the late 14th century. It was given to the family of the last descendants of the Nawab of Awadh in 1985. They stayed in the Mahal till the death of its last royal occupant – Prince Ali Raza in 2017!

Burj Mandal

FASCINATING FORTS

Sketch your favourite fort with its layout and ground plan. What makes this fort unique?

Capital City in Delhi: Tughlaqabad
Dynasty: Tughlaq (Ghiyasud-din Tughlaq) – Delhi Sultanate
Time Period: 14th century

Ghiyasud-din Tughlaq was the founder of the Tughlaq Dynasty. He initially served in the army of Alauddin Khilji as the Governor of the Frontier Province. He came to power after defeating Khusro Khan in 1320-21 and built the city of **Tughlaqabad** after five years of his rule.

Monuments

The Tughlaqabad Fort is a gigantic stone structure in the Aravalli Hills. The fort-city was supposed to have as many as 52 gates, out of which, sadly, only 13 remain. The massive fort with walls that are 3 to 5 metres feet high protected them against the Mongol invasions.

Within the fort premises, Burj or Bijai Mandal was made as a watchtower. Another important feature of Tughlaqabad is the Tomb of Ghiyasud-din. In contrast to the fort, this tomb was made of red sandstone and the dome was made of marble. Next to Ghiyasud-din Tughlaq lie the tombs of his wife, Mukh Dumai Jahan and his son, Muhammad bin Tughlaq.

Ibn Battuta praised the fort in his writings, describing it as being made of gold bricks, which would shine so bright in the sunlight that it would be difficult to look straight at it.

The decline of Tughlaqabad has an interesting legend behind it. Tughlaqabad had a very short lifespan; it was abandoned in less than ten years. Legend says that the reason behind its abandonment is a curse by Nizamuddin Auliya. The Sufi saint and the ruler had an argument over the recruitment of construction workers. Ghiyasud-din made it difficult for Nizamuddin to get a baoli made inside his dargah. In retaliation, the angry Sufi saint cursed the ruler and his fort by saying.

"Ya base Gujar, Ya rahe ujar"
(May it be inhabited by nomadic herders or remain desolate)

Nizamuddin Dargah

THE REFUGE OF THE WORLD

CAPITAL CITY IN DELHI: Jahanpanah
DYNASTY: Tughlaq (Muhammad bin Tughlaq) – Delhi Sultanate
TIME PERIOD: 14th century

In 1324, Muhammad bin Tughlaq came to power and ruled from Tughlaqabad for seven years. To control the Deccan provinces, he whimsically decided to shift the capital to Daulatabad; a journey that proved to be an absolute failure! Upon his return, he built the capital at **Jahanpanah** in 1327, by linking the older cities of Siri and Lal Kot using extensive walled sections and gates.

Monuments

Remains of the city walls of Jahanpanah can be seen in the present day areas of Malviya Nagar, Saket, Panchsheel Park, and Shahpur Jat. The palace complex of the city can be seen in the monument that is called Bijay Mandal. The foundations of royal baths and the zenana have been excavated. The Diwan-i-Khas or the Hall of Private Audience once stood there. Behind the platform, in the Diwan-i-Khas, two stone vaults were found, these were said to be treasure chambers. Gold coins from South India were discovered here. The remains of the Diwan-i-Aam or Public Audience can also be seen. This two-storeyed hall was called the Hall of Thousand Pillars inspired by the one in Alauddin Khilji's Siri.

The Begumpuri Masjid built in the 14th century is located in the middle of the Begumpur village, close to the Bijay Mandal complex. This is often referred to as the Jama Masjid of Jahanpanah. This mosque was probably built by Mohammad bin Tughlaq to serve as the main mosque of Jahanpanah. It was built using Delhi quartzite, and is the second largest mosque in Delhi after Jama Masjid.

Satpula Bridge meaning 'seven spans' was built by Muhammad bin Tughlaq. It is a stone dam with seven arched openings. It was built to regulate the water of the large stream which entered the city of Jahanpanah through the wall at this point.

The Adilabad Fort is adjacent to the Tughlaqabad Fort. Originally, the two were connected by a causeway (a raised road or track across low or wet ground). Built by Muhammad bin Tughlaq in 1327, it was planned and designed on the same lines as Tughlaqabad Fort. It was the fourth fort built in Delhi. Although this fort is mainly in ruins today, the basic structure is still intact.

Dastangoi

Dastangoi or Qissagoi is the art of storytelling from the 13th century. It is said that when Nizamuddin Auliya fell ill, his disciple Amir Khusrau told him a series of stories called the 'Qissa-e-Chahar Dervish' (The Tale of Four Dervishes). Auliya recovered, and this tradition continued.

- Taking any one period of Delhi's history, and a monument as a backdrop, narrate a story in the Dastangoi style.

THE MAD GENIUS

Mohammad bin Tughlaq is often called the 'Mad Tughlaq'. Find out his story and the various changes he implemented during his reign. Was he truly mad or just ahead of his time?

THE CITY OF FIROZABAD

CAPITAL CITY IN DELHI: Firozabad
DYNASTY: Tughlaq (Firoz Shah Tughlaq) – Delhi Sultanate
TIME PERIOD: 14th century

Firoz Shah Tughlaq founded the city of **Firozabad** in 1354, centered around the palace complex called Firoz Shah Kotla. This was one of the first cities to be built on the banks of the Yamuna, partly to solve the problem of water scarcity which was experienced in Tughlaqabad.

DID YOU KNOW ?

According to legend, Firoz Shah Kotla is the Abode of Djinns or Spirits. On Thursdays, people come to offer milk and grain, light candles, and some people even leave written requests.

EDUCATION THEN AND NOW

Describe the traditional education systems of India. Can you find similarities and differences with the education system today?

Monuments

Firoz Shah was very fond of creating masterpieces in architecture. The Pyramid of Cells is probably the most visible structure in Firoz Shah Kotla. It is a pyramidal structure, on top of which the Ashokan Pillar stands.This pillar was brought from Topra in Ambala in 1367. The Jami Masjid here is the congregational mosque. Legend has it that Amir Timur was so impressed with the mosque that he built one along the same lines in Samarkand. The baoli of Firoz Shah Kotla is three storeys deep. The water from the baoli was used to irrigate the gardens of Firoz Shah Kotla.

Firoz Shah was said to be fond of hunting too. Pir Ghaib is a two-storey hunting lodge built near the current Hindu Rao Hospital in the Northern Ridge. Interestingly, the lodge was also used as an observatory. Next to this is the Hindu Rao baoli, also built by Firoz Shah. During the 1857 Revolt, this baoli was the only source of water for the British soldiers as it had a secret tunnel!

Firoz Shah got many buildings restored during his lifetime. Such as the Hauz Khas in 1352. He also built a gate in the Dargah for Roshan Chirag-i-Delhi and built the Dargah Qadam Sharif.

The Madrasa-e-Firoz Shahi in the Hauz Khas complex was one of the famous educational institutions of those times. Learned men, theologians, and teachers would come from across the world to this madrasa.

Firoz Shah Kotla

Another important structure is Firoz Shah's Tomb. Although he died in 1388, he built his tomb around the same time as the madrasa which is attached to the tomb.

THE CITY OF THE SAYYIDS AND LODIS

Capital City in Delhi: Khizrabad
Dynasty: Sayyid and Lodi – Delhi Sultanate
Time Period: 15th-16th century

The Sayyid Dynasty ruled over Delhi from 1414 to 1451. The founder of the Sayyid Dynasty was Khizr Khan, the governor of Multan and Timur's deputy in India. He set up his capital at **Khizrabad** in 1418 along the banks of the Yamuna. They were succeeded by the Lodi (or Lodhi) Dynasty that ruled over Delhi from 1451 to 1526. It was the last dynasty of the Delhi Sultanate and was founded by Bahlol Khan Lodi.

Monuments

Though a garden has existed in this area since the 13th century, Lodi Garden as we know today was developed in 1936 by the British. Initially named Lady Willingdon Park, it was later renamed as Lodi Garden due to its historical and architectural significance.

The best example of Lodi and Sayyid architecture can be seen in the Royal Tombs of Lodi Garden, which are beautiful examples of pre-Mughal architecture in India. Built in 1444, the Tomb of Mohammad Shah from the Sayyid Dynasty is the oldest tomb here. This octagonal-shaped tomb stands on a raised platform. A cluster of small domed chattris surround the main dome and a row of Bottle Palm trees surround the monument. These trees were brought from Cuba in the 1940s. It was during the reign of Sikander Lodi that many of the structures of Lodi Garden took shape. The Bada Gumbad is the largest structure here with an adjoining mosque and rest house on either side. The Sheesh Gumbad, which is opposite the Bada Gumbad, at one point was covered with coloured tiles, of which you can still see the remains. The square building is decorated with floral patterns and inscriptions. The Tomb of Sikander Lodi is located in a square garden, enclosed by walls. There is a mosque on the west side of the tomb.

NATURE WALK

Lodi Garden is not only home to beautiful monuments but also has various species of butterflies, birds and trees.

- Plan a visit to the Lodi Garden.
- Write a story about your visit. Your story must include the names of flora and fauna you observed here.

Tomb of Mohammad Shah Sayyid

The Tomb Story

Royal tombs were usually constructed outside the city and sometimes even before the person's death. According to Islam, the dome formed an essential part of the tomb, symbolizing the sky and was decorated with celestial symbols. Tombs were made in areas closer to those of spiritual leaders and other important people. In the Lodi period, a large number of tombs were constructed and some of these are seen today at the Lodi Gardens.

MONUMENT GAME

This activity will help participants get to know each other better whilst increasing their knowledge about the monuments.

Material Required: Newspapers

Method:

- All the participants would be required to stand in a circle with a piece of newspaper under their feet.
- One person would be standing at the centre of the circle and would introduce herself/himself to others.
- Further he/she would name one monument he/ she has visited in Delhi after saying the phrase 'To all my neighbors who have'.

NOTE: Here we would expect all other participants to swap places with one another if they have visited that monument too. Also, the person at the centre has to grab a spot with the others in the circle quickly. One rule which has to be kept in mind is that the participants cannot swap places with the person standing adjacent to them. The child left without a spot after the swapping of places then has to stand in the centre of the circle.

Bada Gumbad

DID YOU KNOW ?

The Athpula Bridge is located near Sikander Lodi's Tomb. 'Ath' means eight and 'pula' means span or pier. The bridge is said to have been built during the Mughal Emperor Akbar's reign by Nawab Bahadur. The bridge has seven arches and eight piers. This bridge is said to have spanned the tributary of the Yamuna that fed the South Delhi area.

Athpula Bridge

THE CITY OF DINPANAH

Capital City in Delhi: Purana Qila
Dynasty: Mughal (Humayun) and Sur (Sher Shah Suri)
Time Period: 16th century

Babur invaded India, defeating Ibrahim Lodi in the First Battle of Panipat and founded the dynasty of the Great Mughals. His son Humayun ascended the throne after him in 1530. In 1533, he laid the foundation of his city **Dinpanah** (meaning 'asylum of the faith') with the Purana Qila on the banks of the Yamuna. It is believed to have been built on the same site as the legendary city of Indraprastha – the capital of the Pandavas.

Unfortunately, from the beginning, Humayun faced adversities and fought many battles. Sher Shah of the Sur Dynasty successfully defeated Humayun in 1539 and appropriated Dinpanah. He also built his own city and named it Dilli Sher Shahi or Sher Garh. In 1555, Humayun marshalled forces, over powered Sher Shah Suri, and reclaimed Delhi. He further completed some of the structures which were left unfinished by Sher Shah.

Monuments

The Purana Qila Complex is an important landmark of Delhi. It is an oblong octagonal fort. The stone walls of the fort covered a circuit over a mile long and had three impressive gates. The walls were as high as 20 metres and about 4 metres thick.

Purana Qila

MY MONUMENT REPORT

Visit a monument with your friends and identify its main architectural elements. Prepare a questionnaire for the caretaker of the monument and document the details. Here is a sample documentation card.

- Name of the monument
- Date
- Location/Address
- My sketch of the monument
- What is the function of the building?
- Who built it?
- What makes this monument special?
- What are the unique features of the monument?
- Are there any interesting stories or myths associated with the monument?
- What is the present condition of the monument?
  - a) Good
  - b) Needs Improvement
- What are the causes for decay/damage/defacement of the building?
- Any other comments/ suggestions

Other monuments within the complex are –

Sher Mandal

Sher Mandal

It is an octagonal tower, made of red sandstone, probably designed by Sher Shah as a pleasure resort. When Humayun regained power, he converted the Sher Mandal into a library. He died here after a fall from the stairs in 1556 AD.

Baoli

The Purana Qila baoli is a U-shaped baoli which is now kept fenced and locked up. It is 22 metres deep, with 89 narrow steps, punctuated by 8 landings.

The Archaeological Museum

Located within the fort, this hall was part of the original fort. It was later renovated to fit a museum. Many artefacts have been found here – even dating back to the 3rd century BC. The exhibits here trace the history of Delhi from the Mauryan Period till the Mughal Period.

Qila-i-Kohna Masjid

Built by Sher Shah in 1542, the Qila-i-Kohna Masjid stands opposite the Bada Darwaza, described as a 'magnificent mosque'. The façade is decorated with Quranic inscriptions and inlay work carved in sandstone and marble.

Hammam

The Hammam was a relatively newer discovery. It was unearthed only in 1913, when the British were clearing up the area to build modern buildings. It was the bath complex standing next to the Sher Mandal. Some of the earthen pipes can still be seen here.

Gateways

The Purana Qila has three gates: the Humayun Darwaza, Talaqi Darwaza, and Bada Darwaza. It is generally believed that the walls and gates of the Purana Qila were built during the time of Humayun and the mosque and the structure of the Sher Mandal during Sher Shah's period.

Humayun Darwaza

The Matka Peer Story

The Matka Peer Dargah, close to the Purana Qila Complex is from the days of the Slave Dynasty. It is said that to challenge the Sufi Saint Hazrat Sheikh Abu Bakr Tusi Haideri's inner power to perform miracles, the Sultan, Ghiyas ud din Balban sent iron balls and mud to the saint as offerings in pots. After praying, they turned into gram and jaggery, which is what people now offer at the shrine. The dargah has earthen pots (or matkas) hanging from a keekar tree. Matkas are used to give offerings even today.

Humayun's Tomb

Humayun's Tomb Complex

Emperor Humayun died in 1556, after a fall from the steps of his library. His tomb was built between 1565 and 1571, probably by his son Akbar, though sometimes it is credited to his widow Bega Begum, also known as Haji Begum. Humayun's Tomb is the first example of the Persian charbagh style garden tomb. The tomb is at the centre of the intersection of four water channels that run on each side.

The Humayun's Tomb was declared a UNESCO World Heritage Site in 1993. It is one of the most magnificent masterpieces of Mughal architecture. The tomb is built in the sacred area near Hazrat Nizamuddin's dargah. The architect chosen for this was Mirak Mirza Ghiyas from Persia. The Aga Khan Foundation worked for the conservation and restoration of this monument. The process took six years and finished in 2013.

DID YOU KNOW ?

Though it is called the Humayun's Tomb, many others from the Mughal family were also buried here. Due to the absence of inscriptions, however, most of them are unnamed graves. Since so many graves lie here, it is called the 'Dormitory of the House of Timur'.

Double Dome

The dome of this tomb is rather unique. Though it looks humungous from the outside; from the inside, it is well proportionate to the walls and the hall. This is because the dome is actually a double dome, with a gap between them!

Charming Charbagh

The garden which surrounds the Tomb is the Charbagh. It represents the Quranic reference to Paradise. The garden has channels cutting across with water flowing in them and trees beautifying it even further.

Science of Stone

The tomb has been built on a large stone platform, made of red sandstone and marble, while the dome is completely covered in white marble. Different coloured tiles have been used to decorate the chattris and the walls, and the marble walls have carved texts and inlay work.

Jali Geometry

The four sides of the tomb are adorned with jali work on red sandstone. Geometric patterns have been carved on walls, ceiling, and archways for ventilation and entry of sunlight.

HUMAYUN'S EXPERIMENTS

The Mughal Emperor Humayun was an avid astronomer. He is said to have invented a special type of astrolabe. Can you name a few rulers who have invented or developed such scientific instruments? You could start researching on the history of the sun dial too.

Make a unique astronomical instrument of your own using recycled material.

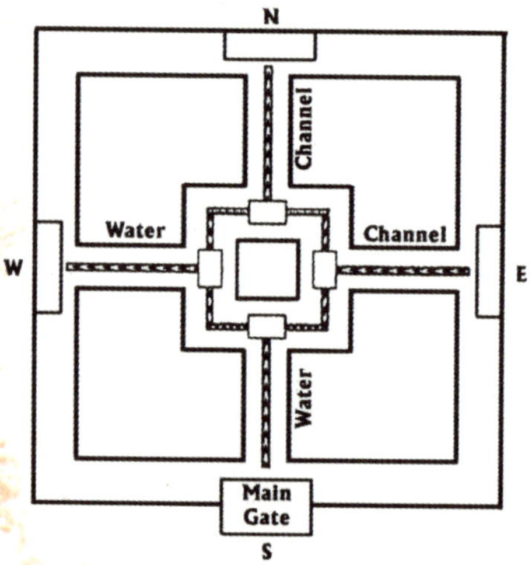

Charbagh (Four-Quartered Garden) Plan

DID YOU KNOW ?

During the 1857 Revolt, the last Mughal Emperor, Bahadur Shah Zafar took refuge at Humayun's Tomb. It was at this tomb complex that he surrendered to the British.

Inside a walled enclosure within the Humayun's Tomb Complex stands a mosque and the Tomb of Isa Khan, who was a nobleman in the court of Sher Shah Suri. Both these monuments were built at least 20 years before the Humayun's Tomb.

Barber's Tomb is a domed square tomb, built in 1590, lying diagonally across the Humayun's Tomb. It has chattris with green-blue tiles and is decorated with arches and jalis. According to popular legend, this tomb was given to a barber as he held immense power by holding a razor to the emperor's throat everyday!

The Garden of Bu Halima marks the entrance of the Humayun's Tomb. Nothing is known of her, but it is said that she could have been Humayun's wet nurse. The wall of Bu Halima's Garden was broken in the middle to allow easy access to the main tomb complex.

The Tomb of Afsarwala is also situated within this enclosure. It was probably built by a Mughal officer but the identity is unknown. A small mosque stands close to it on the same platform. Both the structures are built in a simple and bold style.

According to one theory, Arab ki Sarai was built for the purpose of housing and was named after the 300 Arabs who Hamida Begum brought back from Mecca. Another theory was that this Sarai was built to house the artists working on the Humayun's Tomb Complex. Today, very little remains of it.

LOOKING THROUGH THE JALI

The jali is a beautiful Mughal contribution to architecture. They allowed air and light to flow through the structure. The unique feature of these jalis was that they were carved out of one single stone slab. At Humayun's Tomb, no two jali designs are the same!

Make a bookmark using your own jali pattern and colour it.

THE CITY OF OLD DELHI

Capital City in Delhi: Shahjahanabad
Dynasty: Mughal (Shahjahan)
Time Period: 17th century

After Humayun, during the reign of Akbar, the Imperial capital shifted to Agra and then to Lahore under Jahangir. In 1639, Shahjahan ordered the construction of a new city at Delhi called **Shahjahanabad**, and shifted the capital from Lahore to Delhi in 1648, when it was inaugurated. A canal system, linked to the Yamuna, was laid for water requirements. The symbolic focus of the city was the Red Fort, the Imperial Residence.

Monuments

The massive Red Fort Complex is made of red sandstone. It took almost a decade to get completed (1639–1648). The fort is enclosed by a stone wall with bastions and gates. It was the seat of the Mughal Dynasty for over 200 years. In 1837, the last Mughal Emperor Bahadur Shah Zafar was coronated here. At that time, however, his powers did not extend beyond the boundaries of his palace.

Red Fort Complex

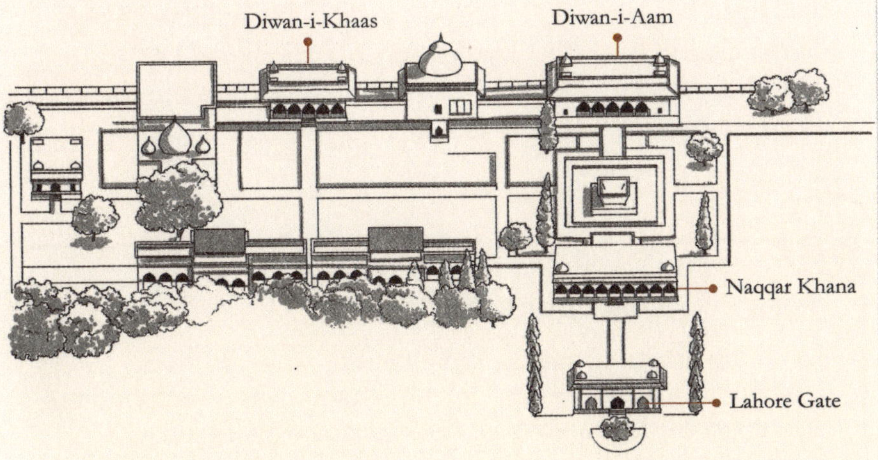

DID YOU KNOW ?

The Hammam here was not just the emperor's bathhouse; many important state matters were often discussed here with the courtiers.

Diwan-i- Aam

Diwan-i-Aam was the place where the emperor heard the grievances of the common people. The royal throne stood here under a marble canopy. The wall behind the throne was decorated with beautiful panels of pietra dura work of trees, flowers, and birds.

Naqqar Khana

The Naqqar Khana marks the entrance to the Diwan-i-Aam and was originally used as a music gallery. Musicians would play the drums to mark special occasions like the birthday of the emperor. Now, it has been converted into a War Memorial Museum.

Nahrr-i-Behisht

Nahrr-i-Behisht or the 'Stream of Paradise' is seen running through the centers of all the pavilions constructed in the fort. This water was fed by the Yamuna through the Shah Burj that stands in the north-eastern corner of the Red Fort, using a hydraulic system.

Diwan-i-Khaas

The Diwan-i-Khaas is the Hall of Private Audience. The hall was made completely of marble. Its marble dias is said to have supported the famous Peacock Throne which was taken away by the Persian invader Nadir Shah.

Private Palaces

The Khaas Mahal was the private palace of the Emperor, decorated with carved marble work. The Rang Mahal was the chief building for the Imperial harem. Hira Mahal was a simple structure built during the reign of Bahadur Shah II who was living on a pension given by the East India Company.

Jama Masjid

Jama Masjid, the congregational mosque, was an important focal point of the city. It was patronized by Emperor Shahjahan himself. It was a royal mosque where the emperor would come to pray. Built on a natural hillock, it stands 10 metres above the level of the city. Though its layout is similar to the other congregational mosques in Delhi which were built before it, this mosque is much grander in size, with overpowering magnificence.

The other very important mosque of Shahjahanabad is the Fatehpuri Masjid. It was built by Fatehpuri Begum, Shahjahan's wife. Closer to the Daryanganj area, one will also find the Zinat-ul-Masjid, built by one of Emperor Aurangzeb's daughters.

Razia Sultan's Tomb lies almost forgotten on the streets of Old Delhi, near Turkman Gate. She was the daughter of Iltutmish of the Slave Dyansty and the only woman ruler of Medieval Delhi. How the Empress died is still a mystery! The tomb consists of four walls without a roof, and two graves; one of Raziya and the other maybe of her sister, Sajiya.

Gurudwara Sisganj in Chandni Chowk commemorates the spot where the ninth Guru, Tegh Bahadur was killed on the orders of Emperor Aurangzeb at the Mughal police station (or Kotwal) which stood here.

Sri Digambar Jain Lal Mandir was built as a temple for the Jains in the city of Shahjahanabad, many of whom were given land in nearby Dariba to set up their business houses. Now, a bird hospital stands behind the temple.

DID YOU KNOW ?

Every year on India's Independence Day (15th August), the Prime Minister of India hoists the national flag at the Red Fort and delivers a nationally-broadcast speech from its ramparts.

Red Fort

INDO-ISLAMIC ARCHITECTURE

With the arrival of the Delhi Sultanate, a new form of architecture – Indo-Islamic architecture – was developed blending Central and West Asian styles with Indian ones. Elements such as arches, domes, minars, and jalis became characteristic features of this style. Looking at the following illustrations, draw similar sketches.

Dome

Arch

Minar

Bustling Bazaars

Chandni Chowk was originally the name given to a beautiful city square built by Princess Jahanara. In the centre of the square was a large pool. It is said that on a moonlit night, the pool used to shimmer, throwing bright reflections on the complex, and as a result, it acquired the name of Chandni Chowk or 'moonlight square'. Today, this name has been given to the whole street that runs westwards from the Red Fort, and sometimes even to the nearby areas.

There are many markets in the city of Shahjahanabad. Dariba Kalan specializes in the sale of silver and gold items. Kinari Bazar deals in laces, sequins, zari borders and much more. Chawri Bazar deals in paper and metal products, Katra Neel was named after indigo, which was used to dye fabrics. Nowadays, dyeing does not take place here, but it remains a market for cloth. Khari Baoli was the traditional spice market which played a major role in foreign trade. People still throng to this street for the choicest of spices!

Daryaganj, an important locality in North Delhi, was a part of the walled city of Shahjahanabad. In those days, it used to be known as Faiz Bazar and it was a vibrant commercial place. The name Daryaganj, originates from 'darya' which literally means river, in reference to the Yamuna beside which it was situated.

Harmonious Havelis

Havelis are a type of home that can be seen in Shahjahanabad – now Old Delhi. Many of these can be dated back to the Medieval Period, and were inhabited by the noblity and merchants. However, it is sad to see that today most of these residential structures stand in ruins. Some well-known havelis are Ghalib's Haveli, Zeenat Mahal, Haveli Chunna Mal, among many others.

DID YOU KNOW ?

Haveli Bhawani Shankar was built by the man after whom it is named. It is more popularly known as Namak Haram ki Haveli. This is because Bhawani Shankar was not true to his salt. He had abandoned the Marathas and switched over to the British side in 1803.

SILVER STREETS OF CHANDNI CHOWK

"You have come out from the cloud-capped towers, out from the royal palaces – and here lies the Silver Street. Every shop is stocked with goods that would certainly impress a European. They are filled with rich spices, cloth, perfumes, pietra-dura, sculptures, pots etc..."

Extract from essay by Farhan Bhakt Ahmed, Modern School, Barakhamba Road

- Do a comparative study of markets then and now.
- Discuss how street markets are a symbol of secularism and unity.

* Popular Hindi Tongue Twister
Translation – On a full moon night in Chandni Chowk, Chandu's uncle made Chandu's aunt taste a spoonful of chutney in a silver spoon.

LUTYENS DELHI

DID YOU KNOW ?

The British monarchs had laid the foundation of the new capital at Kingsway Camp. However, Lutyens and Baker felt that Raisina Hill was a more suitable site. The contractor, Sir Sobha Singh, thus, relocated the foundation stones to Raisina Hill. This was done under cover of darkness, to avoid bad luck.

Capital City in Delhi: New Delhi
Dynasty: British Rule
Time Period: 19th -20th century

"I have always said, and continue to say, that I want to see at Delhi, a fine and broad style of architecture with Indian tradition and sentiment running throughout..."

Lord Hardinge, Viceroy, *Dome over India*

In 1803, the British East India Company conquered Delhi. They became the actual rulers of Delhi, while the Mughal emperors continued to live in the Red Fort as puppet rulers. This continued till 1857, when the last Mughal Emperor was exiled and the British Crown took over. All this was done while the British ruled India not from Delhi – but Calcutta. However, Delhi retained symbolic importance. In 1911, a Durbar was held in Delhi, and King George V, the newly crowned emperor announced the shift of the Imperial capital from Calcutta to Delhi. Two British architects, Edwin Lutyens and Herbert Baker designed some of the important buildings of **New Delhi**. Though the work had begun in 1912, the city was only inaugurated in 1931, as construction was delayed due to World War I. The architectural style was European with many Indian features too.

Geometry of New Delhi

Lutyens enjoyed using geometrical shapes in his designs. It was reflected in elements in his plan for New Delhi as well.

- A **hexagon system** with separate triangular sections was created. Important buildings were built at these intersections.
- A **rectangular central avenue**, known as Rajpath (earlier Kingsway), was designed as a processional path that linked the Viceroy's House or Rashtrapati Bhavan to the War Memorial Arch or India Gate.

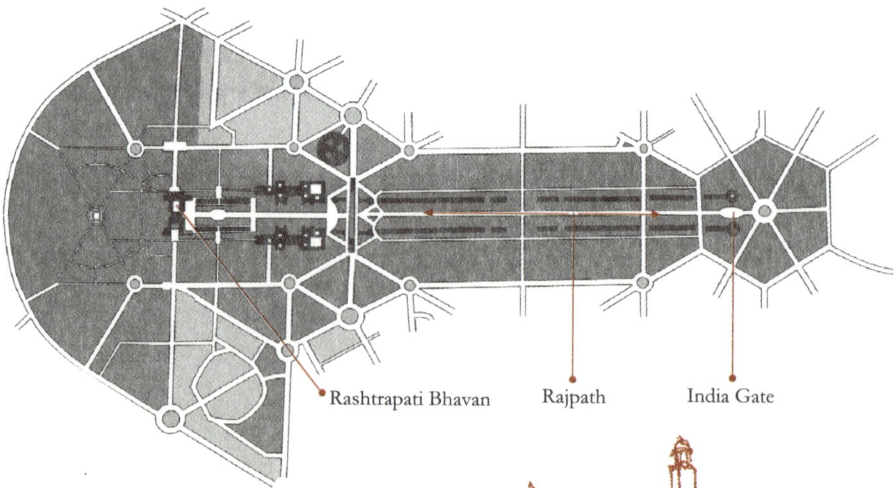

Rashtrapati Bhavan

Monuments

Rashtrapati Bhavan is perhaps one of the most impressive structures in India located on the western end of Rajpath. The older rulers had already taken all the favourable locations in Delhi to create their own cities. There was no place left for the British capital. The town planners surveyed the area thoroughly to find an ideal site and finally, in 1912, Lord Hardinge decided that the Viceroy's House should be built on Raisina Hill. Following Independence, the Viceroy's House became Rashtrapati Bhavan, the official residence of the President of India.

The Rashtrapati Bhavan is a part of a truly regal Presidential complex with many structures, beautified using the most superior architectural materials and elements inspired by Indian, Western, as well as Mughal building practices.

The **dome** was inspired by the domes of St. Paul's Cathedral and the Sanchi Stupa.

The **pillars** are a combination of the Indian temple architecture and the Greek and Roman pillar styles.

The **chattri**, a domed pavilion, was used by Lutyens, he upturned some of them, to make fountain bowls which one can see on the façade of the building.

The **jali** design was used for ventilation, and gentle, filtered sunlight.

The **chhajja** is a projecting stone slab that protects the wall from the hot sun and the rain.

DID YOU KNOW ?

In July 2014, a Museum inside the Rashtrapati Bhavan's grounds was inaugurated by the then President of India, Pranab Mukherjee. The museum aims at giving an inside view of the building's history, occupants, art, and architecture.

Durbar Hall

The Durbar Hall lies right under the dome and was the main hall where official functions were held. In this room, Dr. Rajendra Prasad was sworn in as the first President of India.

Ashok Hall

The Ashok Hall was originally planned as the State Ballroom and is now used for formal gatherings.

Fit for The President

The Rashtrapati Bhavan has 340 rooms, 227 columns, and 37 fountains. Fit for the President of the world's largest democracy!

Cabinet Room

The Cabinet Room is filled with bookshelves and a large map depicting the marine and air routes of India with the world. The President holds his meetings in this room.

Mughal Garden

The Mughal Garden, famous for its roses, was inspired by the Persian design of the charbagh. The gardens are opened to the public annually.

DID YOU KNOW ?

Lutyens wanted a gentle slope for the Viceroy's House – so as to ensure the building remained in sight. However, Baker insisted on building it on a steep slope. A disagreement over this led to the end of a trusted friendship. Baker described the episode as the "the unhappiest in all my life's work" and Lutyens referred to it as his "bitterest memory of India"!

ARTY ARCHITECTURE

Do some research about the various architectural elements, such as dome, jali, arches, and others. Find a continuity in their usage in Delhi's architecture from the Medieval Period to the Modern.

Which is your favourite building in New Delhi? Give three reasons for your selection.

Write an account of your visit to New Delhi – maybe to Rashtrapati Bhavan or to observe the Republic Day Parade.

Parliament House

In 1921, Herbert Baker designed the Council House – a circular building in the Secretariat Complex. Its foundation stone was laid by the Duke of Connaught. Later, the name was changed to the Parliament House or the Sansad Bhavan. The two houses of the Parliament – Lok Sabha and Rajya Sabha – are located here.

The Parliament House was built on a red sandstone platform, 170.6 metres in diameter, with a dome. The circular building has a corridor, lined with approximately 144 pillars which are 8 metres high.

It has a striking resemblance to the Chausath Yogini temple in Jabalpur, Madhya Pradesh. It is said that it might have been an inspiration for the architects.

Herbert Baker designed the Central Secretariat – the primary offices of the British Empire. These were two blocks of symmetrical buildings (North Block and South Block). Today, it houses key ministries of the Indian Government.

One of the most important structures of the new capital was the 'All India War Memorial Arch' now known as India Gate. Situated near the end of Kingsway or Rajpath, it was designed by Edwin Lutyens, completed in 1931. The arch of the building was inspired by the Arc de Triomphe de l' Étoile in Paris. It was built in the memory of soldiers who died in World War I and other wars fought for the British. An eternal flame – the 'Amar Jawan Jyoti' lit in their honour pays tribute to them. In 2019, the National War Memorial was built near India Gate, to honour India's Armed Forces.

India Gate

DELHI TODAY

CAPITAL CITY IN DELHI: Modern Delhi
AFTER INDEPENDENCE; TIME PERIOD: 1947 onwards

Post Independence architecture was characterized by continued use of past architectural styles combined with newer elements, material, and technology. Well-known contractor and real estate builder, Sir Sobha Singh was involved in making many buildings for **Modern Delhi** such as, Connaught Place, All India Radio, National Museum.

Modern Buildings

There are many iconic architecture dominating the city's landscape which are worth a mention:

The Ashok Hotel was designed by B.E. Doctor (a Mumbai based architect) and was opened to the public in 1956. It was commissioned to host the IX UNESCO Conference in Delhi by Jawaharlal Nehru. It is believed that Nehru used to tour the property and oversee its construction on horseback.

The LIC building (in Connaught Place) was designed by Charles Correa in 1986. It gave a distinctive feature to Delhi's architecture. The use of red sandstone (inspired by the Red Fort) on the otherwise glass skyscraper is a unique feature of this building.

LIC Building

Lotus Temple

The Lotus Temple or the Baha'i House of Worship, designed by Fariborz Sahba was built in 1986. Designed in the shape of a lotus, it brings out elements of purity, simplicity and freshness of the Baha'i faith. The faith was founded in the 19th century with the goal to unite people into one global family.

The Akshardham Temple, a spiritual and cultural campus (including a temple complex, gardens, exhibitions, and a water show), was built in 2005. Akshardham means the 'divine abode of God'. The temple is made of pink sandstone and marble. It is dedicated to Bhagwan Swaminarayan, devas, and great sages of Hinduism.

Stein Story

Joseph Allen Stein, a well known American architect designed several buildings in Delhi, especially in Lodi Estate. Therefore, this area is often referred to as *'Steinabad'*. In fact, the Joseph Stein Lane – named after him, is perhaps the only street in Delhi named after an architect! His designs, though contemporary, incorporated some medieval architectural elements like jalis. He used earthy colours and achieved an ecological balance by maintaining harmony with nature in his architecture. Some buildings designed by him are the India International Center (IIC), India Habitat Center (IHC) and Triveni Kala Sangam.

AMAZING ARCHITECTURE

Select any building in your city and find out the following details:

- Name of the building, location, and date
- Architect/ Patron of the building
- Function
- Building materials
- Condition of the building
- Caretaker of the building

DID YOU KNOW ?

Sarai Kale Khan – now an urban village, used to be a Gujjar farming village and was a sarai or inn built by a late Mughal-era nobleman called 'Kale Khan'.

EMBASSY ARCHITECTURE

Shantipath is the main road in the diplomatic area of Chanakyapuri. Many embassies are located here. Some architecturally remarkable embassies are the American, Belgian, Swedish, and Royal Bhutanese embassies.

- Find out the architects of these structures, the styles used and whether it is a green building or not.
- Design your own green building and describe its concept, purpose, and materials used.

Urban Villages

After Independence, accelerated urbanization with population growth led to the expansion of the city into adjoining villages and transformation of the rural spaces. Delhi is a classic example of urbanization with several surrounding villages becoming a part of its urban landscape. These villages can be referred to as 'urban villages'.

Some examples are:

Kotla Mubarak (in existence since 1500) was a medieval village. It is now a residential colony.

Munirka, once a village in the outer fringe of Metropolitan Delhi, has been enveloped by residential colonies like Rama Krishna Puram, Vasant Vihar, and DDA flats.

Lado Sarai sandwiched in the layers of the first cities of Delhi (Lal Kot and Mehrauli), is an urban village that has become an art hub.

ADOPT A MONUMENT

Adopting a monument has become a need of the hour. As heritage enthusiasts, we can come together and take this heritage awareness movement forward. Some things to do:

- Adopt a historical building as a group
- Take the assistance of the INTACH Chapter, Archaeological Survey of India, State Archaeology etc.
- Ensure it is maintained and kept clean
- Spread awareness about the monument by giving out information sheets, having exhibitions about the monument, and organizing walks
- Identify the main custodians/stakeholders of the selected monument
- Engage with the local community and make them a part of your heritage movement
- Make a panel of Monument Monitors for follow-up activities

ARCHITECTURAL MARVELS

Entry Points to The City – *Beautiful Gates*

Gateways served as an entry point to a city and often signalled towards a newly conquered region. They were also designed to inspire awe, grandeur, and convey declaration of victory as well as support the kingdom's defence. Each city of Delhi built different gates. However, only a few are in a good condition. The remaining are in ruins.

- The first city of Lal Kot had seven gates. Among these, the Chaumukha, the Ranjit, the Sohan and, the Fateh Darwazas have been listed as heritage monuments or structures by INTACH.
- The second city of Siri had seven gates. However, only the Southeastern gate remains.
- When the city of Tughlaqabad was built, it had 52 gates. However, only 13 remain. Among these gates, the fort's main entry gate was built in red sandstone.
- Shahjahanabad, the seventh city of Delhi was built by Shah Jahan. It was designed like a fortress encircled by strong and high red–brick walls with 14 entry gates. Among the 14 gates, only five gates have survived. These are Kashmiri Gate (in the north), Ajmeri Gate (in the south-west), Delhi Gate (in the south-east), Turkman Gate (in the south), and Nigambodh Gate (in the north-east).

The Walled City

Shahjahanabad is often referred to as the Walled City. It had 14 gates, of which two were part of the Red Fort – The Lahori Gate and the Delhi Gate.

GLORIOUS GATE

Imagine you are a Mughal ruler who has conquered an important region in the Indian subcontinent. Design a gate that would announce your victory. What would you name the gate? In a calligraphic style, write your own personalised inscription for this glorious gate.

Delhi Gate

Humayun Darwaza

Sarai Story

Well-known sarais that are an important part of Delhi's landscape are Lado Sarai, Katwaria Sarai, Yusuf Sarai, Sheikh Sarai, Kalu Sarai, Jia Sarai, Ber Sarai, and Sarai Kale Khan.

The ruins of Badli-ki-Sarai in North Delhi was once a travellers' inn. It is now remembered as the site where 'the Battle of Badli ki Sarai' was fought during the revolt of 1857.

Jasola Kos Minar

Journey to The City – *Kos Minars and Sarais*

'Kos' is an ancient Indian unit for distance and 'Minar' is the persian word for pillar. Kos minars were strategically erected by Mughal Emperors on highways to mark distance and facilitate navigation. Apart from this, they served as a mechanism for communication with horsemen delivering 'shahi daak' or 'royal posts', almost like a modern day speed-post!

Over time, the kos minars disappeared, however, some traces of their existence remain in few sites such as, Badarpur, Jasola Vihar, Faridabad, the Delhi Zoo, and Mathura road in Delhi. In addition, Kos Minars were also on India's old highways, particularly, the Grand Trunk Road.

A Sarai was an inn or a resting place, where travellers would retreat during their journey. Sarais were built across Delhi during the Medieval Period. In the 18th century, a sarai was built near Khari Baoli in Delhi by Bibi Saheba. She was the wife of Mohammad Khan Bangash and the sarai built by her was called Bangash ki Serai. In 1650, Jahanara Begum commissioned the construction of a sarai called Begumabad. Today, the Town Hall in Chandni Chowk stands where the sarai once existed.

SOJOURN AT THE SARAI

List some sarais in Delhi. Imagine you are a traveller from the Medieval Period and describe your stay at a sarai in Delhi.

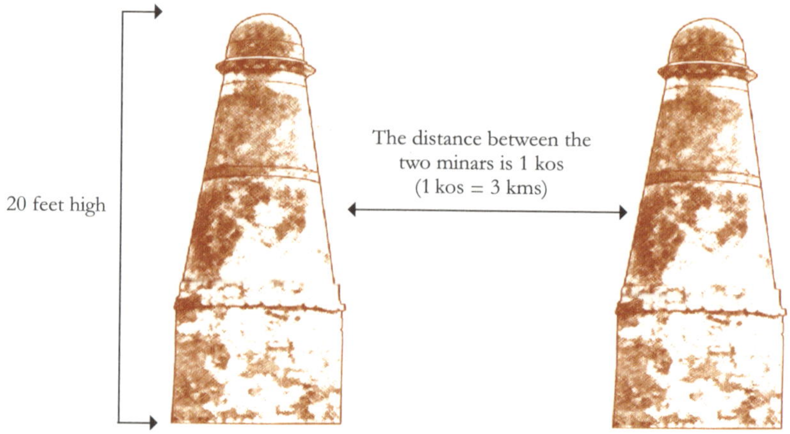

Water Wisdom – *Baolis*

Agrasen ki Baoli

A Baoli or a Step-well was a man-made reservoir used to store water. They usually had a series of steps leading to ground water. The construction of baolis was commissioned by various emperors, in and around Delhi.

Agrasen ki Baoli was built by a legendary Raja Agrasen who lived in the ancient town of Agroha (Haryana). However, there is no official record to verify the account. The well as we know it today, was restored by the Agarwal community in the 14th century.

Gandhak ki Baoli in Mehrauli is among the oldest baolis in Delhi. It was built during the period of Iltutmish for the Sufi Saint Bakhtiyar Kaki. It is believed when Iltutmish visited the saint, he noticed that he had not bathed for days as he did not have a suitable place. Therefore, Iltutmish commissioned the construction of a step-well for the saint enabling him to bathe and access the site without any difficulty. It is called Gandhak ki baoli because of the smell of sulphur (gandhak) in its water. Another name of this five-tiered baoli is 'Diving Well' as youngsters often enjoy taking a jump and dive into it!

Baoli of Nizamuddin Auliya is inside Nizamuddin Auliya's Dargah. Once known as Chashma Dilkusha ('heart uplifting spring'), the baoli is surrounded by walls on three sides, with steps built on the north side down to the level of the water. The baoli was constructed under the supervision of Hazrat Nizamuddin and its water was therefore believed to be sacred with curative powers.

Other important baolis of Delhi are Rajon ki Baoli, Hindu Rao Baoli, the Baolis at Purana Qila and Firoz Shah Kotla.

DID YOU KNOW ?

The use of baolis or step-wells discontinued due to breeding of gineau worms (water-borne parasites) that caused an epidemic in Delhi. Fortunately, there are hardly any cases of this disease today.

Dwarka Discovery

In 2010-2011, a 16th century baoli from the Lodi Dynasty was discovered in Dwarka. ASI, in partnership with INTACH, were involved in its restoration.

CATCH THE RAIN!

References to water harvesting can be found throughout Indian history.

- Study the need for rain water harvesting. Discuss its importance and relevance today.
- In groups, choose one historical water harvesting site in Delhi. Understand its background – when, why, and by whom was it constructed.
- Think of ways in which rainwater can be collected easily.
- Construct a rain water harvesting unit in your locality.

Heritage Homes – *Havelis*

A Haveli refers to a residential complex with a courtyard, ornamental gateways, arched entrances, jharokhas, and columns. In Shahjahanabad, the havelis were inhabited by nobility, and gatherings with music or dance performances organised here.

In Old Delhi, walking down Balliram Lane, you will find Ghalib's Haveli – India's famous poets and an important poet in the court of Bahadur Shah Zafar II. The haveli was presented to Ghalib by a hakim (traditional physician) who was an ardent admirer of his poetry. Here, Ghalib wrote some of his finest ghazals and recited them to a large audience. Today, the haveli is under the jurisdiction of ASI and houses a memorial museum.

Kala Mahal built by Mughal Emperor Shah Jahan was used as his residence temporarily (before the completion of the Red Fort). After Partition, the palace was bought by moneylender and trader Chunna Mal. Lala Rai Chunna Mal was a wealthy moneylender and textile trader of Old Delhi in the 1800s. He owned a large portion of Chandni Chowk and lived there too. His haveli built in 1848, continues to be a landmark in Chandni Chowk. It is a beautiful mansion with intricate artwork and exquisite chandeliers hanging from the high ceilings. It remains well-preserved till date.

Zeenat Mahal is a run-down forgotten haveli of Lal Kuan Street. As the name suggests, it was constructed by the Empress Zeenat Mahal in 1846.

Haveli of Begum Samru was a palatial four-storeyed structure made of stone and marble. It is built with a blend of Greek, Roman, and Mughal architectural styles. Today, it is called Bhagirath Palace and is surrounded by a market.

Restored Haveli

Dharampura Haveli (in Chandni Chowk) was built in Late Mughal architectural style in 1887. The ground floor was for commercial purposes, while the subsequent floors were for residential purposes.

The haveli was restored recently and operates as a heritage hotel now. It gives immense hope to other havelis that could transform with an architectural-restorative-makeover!

ARCHITECTS IN THE MAKING

Visit a monument and identify a particular architectural element you like. Write what the monument symbolizes, its purpose, and its various architectural features.

Living Heritage

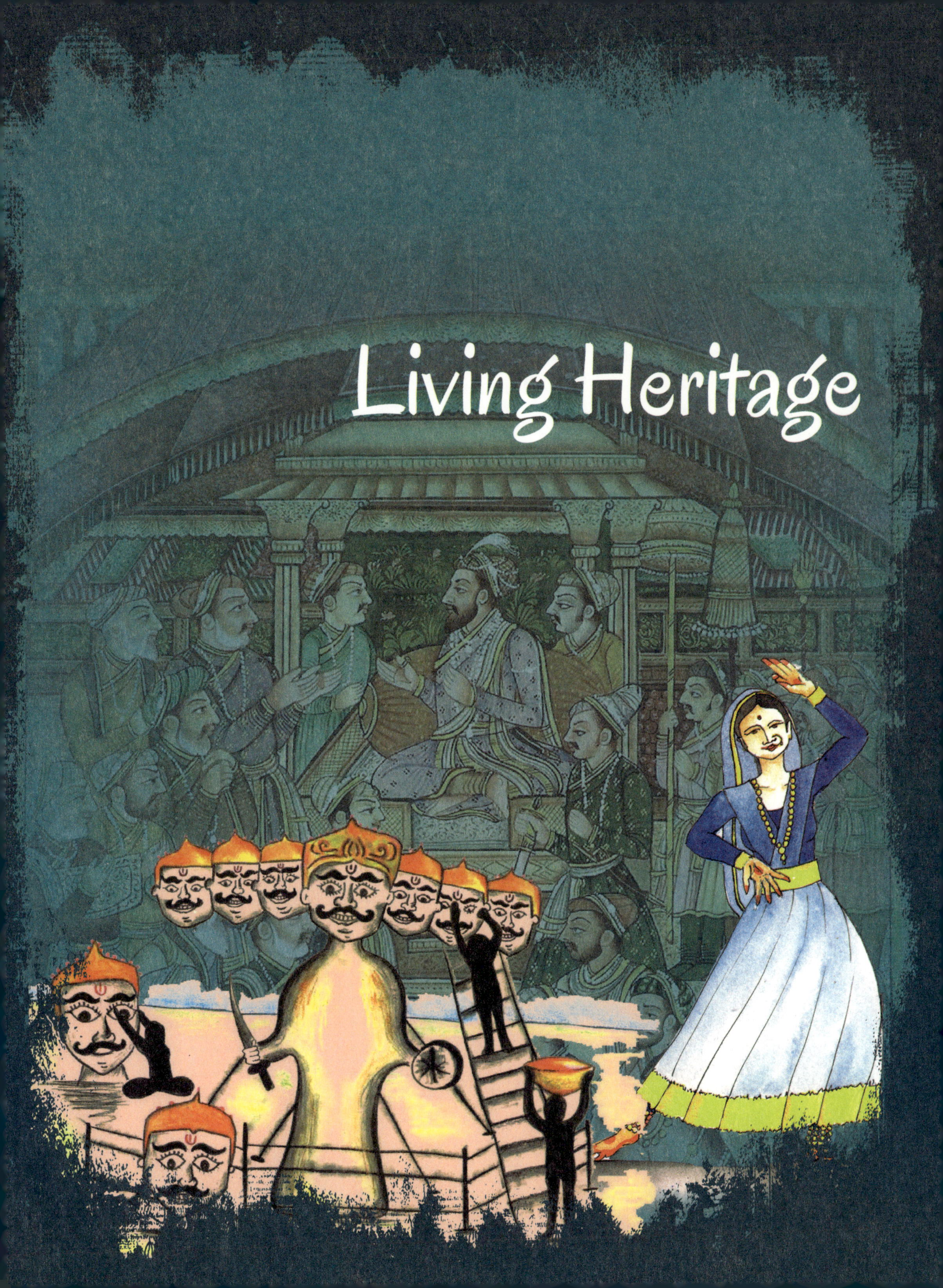

PERFORMING ARTS

MY LIVING ICON

Collect photographs of artists, musicians, singers, and dancers associated with Delhi. Find out about their childhood, training, and their life as 'cultural icons'. Prepare a scrapbook about their life and interesting stories about the performing arts they practise.

The arts have been patronized by the rulers of Delhi and have been an important aspect of the city's cultural life. Initially, performances were viewed by an audience comprising of rulers, aristocrats, administrators, and the elite. Today, however, the audience comprises of people from all walks of life.

Let us examine some art forms thriving in the city...

Theatre

A historic theatre or story-telling tradition is Dastangoi. The word 'Dastangoi' literally means 'to tell a tale'. It was a form of story-telling set in the Medieval Period with story-tellers or the 'dastangos' sitting on the floor and narrating a story in poetic Urdu. An interesting feature of Dastangoi was the absence of props. It is believed, that every Thursday, the 'dastangos' would gather on the steps of Jama Masjid and narrate their dastaans. These stories were about magic, djinns, and prophecies, surrounding the character of Hamza – who was believed to be the Uncle of Prophet Mohammed. Currently, efforts have been made to revive the dying art form and bring it back to popular memory.

Ravana effigy, Dusshera

Traditionally, the annual Ramlila takes place at the Ramlila grounds during Dusshera. It continues to attract people and is an important part of the city's theatre scene. Ramlila performances also take place at Subash Maidan near the Red Fort market. The Shriram Bhartiya Kala Kendra Theatre, near Mandi House, is a well-known Indian cultural institute that has been showcasing a Kathak-based Ramlila annually since 1957. It also runs a school for music, dance and performing arts in New Delhi.

After Independence, once the nationalistic sentiments swelled, theatre came to the forefront. It now enjoys popular awakening throughout the country and Delhi has become a hub for interesting theatre events. The National School of Drama (NSD) hosts an annual theatre festival – Bharat Rang Mahotsav. Mandi House has many centres that host cultural events as well.

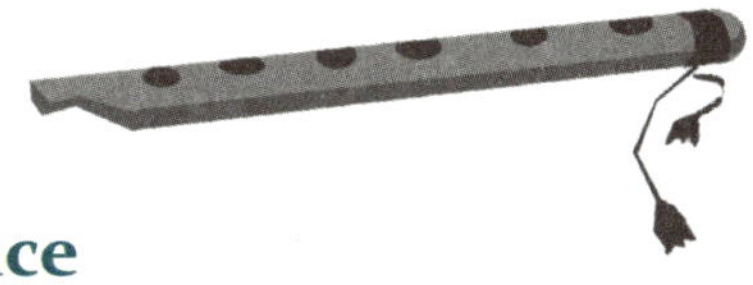

Music and Dance

Firoz Shah Tughlaq, among the orthodox rulers from the Delhi Sultanate, was believed to be a patron of music. Rulers of the Sur Dynasty were patrons of music too.

Khayal is a popular form of Hindustani Classical music. This is represented by a number of Gharanas, one of the most prominent being the Dilli Gharana. Founded in the 18th century, its origins can be traced back to the Delhi Sultanate. According to legends, it is believed that two brothers, Niamat Khan and Feroz Khan from Delhi, known as Sadarang and Adarang – who were not in the good books of the Emperor Muhammad Shah Rangile – created this new form of singing and presented it to the Emperor to win back his favour. Since then, this form of music holds an important space in the cultural landscape of Delhi.

Kathak dance was appreciated by the Mughal rulers. It developed, evolved, and inculcated the tastes of the Mughal courts and was performed for an aristocratic audience. During the British rule, this dance form declined but its prominence has grown since Independence.

While newer forms of music and dance are coming up, old classical forms have kept their hold. Today, organizations like SPIC MACAY work towards bringing classical forms of music and dance back to the forefront. They work with schools and try to inculcate a love for the classical arts among the youth. The Gandharva Mahavidyala established in 1939 has helped popularise Indian classical music and dance.

Kathak Dance

DID YOU KNOW ?

Qawwali is a popular music form associated with Sufism. It is a fusion of devotional poetry and Hindustani music developed by poet and mystic, Amir Khusrau. Even today, at the dargah (shrine) of the Sufi saint Hazrat Nizamuddin Auliya in Delhi, qawwali is performed every Thursday.

Artists in Delhi

Till date, Delhi is home to a number of artists practicing varying arts – musicians and dancers who have added to the diversity of Delhi's modern culture. They continue to be our cultural pride. Well-known artists in Delhi are Amjad Ali Khan, Yamini Krishnamurthy, Shovana Narayan, Iqbal Ahmad Khan, Sonal Mansingh, Shubha Mudgal and many more.

Unique Show!

Akshardham Temple has a Sahaj Anand Water Show that uses lights, sounds, and fountains to depict a story about the innocence of children challenging the power of the Gods. The story has been adapted from the Kena Upanishad – a Vedic Sanskrit text.

A CULTURAL EXPERIENCE

Attend and document a cultural festival in your city, such as a literature or a storytelling festival.

- Name the festival.
- Where did it take place?
- Famous personalities that spoke or performed.
- What was a unique and striking feature of the festival?

Cultural Festivals

Delhi is an eclectic amalgamation of culture and heritage. Since the 16th century, Phoolwalon-ki Sair, a procession of flowers has been observed in Delhi. People carry flowers and floral fans to the Yogmaya Temple and the shrine of the Sufi saint Khwaja Qutbuddin Bakhtiar Kaki. Kite flying festival is celebrated on Makar Sankranti at Connaught Place in January. Amir Khusrau's anniversary is celebrated with a qawwali and sufi music festival in April.

Many historical sites, like the Purana Qila, Siri Fort, Qutub Minar are venues for art and cultural events, like classical dance, music performances, festivals and more recently, light and sound shows. Along with heritage walks, books, pamphlets, the light and sound shows have become a creative and interesting way of showcasing a monument and its history, such as the ones organised at the Red Fort and Purana Qila.

Delhi has hosted a number of art festivals where artists from various places display their works. Over the past few years, Delhi has been hosting many literature festivals too, wherein, literature enthusiasts interact with authors and literary personalities. Food and other cuisine festivals are important to highlight the diverse cultures of the various regions in our country. Contemporary forms of storytelling are growing too and are also organised into festivals attended by children and adults.

ARTS AND CRAFTS

It is difficult to imagine life without art! Historically, rulers would commission artists to make art-works and paintings for them. **Miniature paintings** were initially made on palm leaves and later on paper. In the 16th century, under the Mughals, the subjects of these paintings shifted to matters of the court and thus included portraits, court, and palace scenes. A great collection of miniatures can be found at the National Museum of Delhi. During the Company Rule, the tradition of paintings continued and portraits of officers were painted. As they explored India, they wanted to capture the exotic people, unusual flora and fauna, and the exquisite monuments. For this, the painters used watercolours and techniques of linear perspective and shading.

However, art was not restricted merely to paintings. Artists were commissioned to beautify and illustrate books. They would make designs and illustrations as well as write in various calligraphic styles. Calligraphy was regarded as a form of craft for which people were especially trained. Art from this period may be seen in the grand architecture and intricate carvings on the walls of many monuments.

Delhi was also famous for ivory carvings, and some specimens can be found in the Red Fort Archaeological Museum. The Mughal rulers popularised crafts such as, marble carvings, glass engraving, meenakari work, carpet making, and enamelling as well. They enabled craftsmen to grow which further helped popularise their craft.

Miniature painting style

DID YOU KNOW?

Extracts from natural resources were used to prepare colours for Miniature paintings. These included, minerals, vegetables, precious stones, and conch shells. The paintings would be rubbed on smooth stones to give a smooth and shiny look. Thereafter, decorations with crushed gold and silver colour were added to give it a regal look!

Coins and Calligraphy

Coinage from the Medieval Period, especially the Delhi Sultanate reflect metallurgical expertise. Coins often had the names of spiritual heads and Quranic verses in beautiful calligraphy. Under the Mughal Emperor Jahangir, zodiacal signs and portraits ornamented the coins too.

Craft Clusters

The **Prajapati colony** is the biggest potters' colony in Delhi, home to almost 700 potter families. The potters here create their products from raw material which are then fired into finished products.

The **Kathputhali colony** of Delhi is a well-known colony of street performers. It was established by Rajasthani puppeteers from where the colony received its name.

DID YOU KNOW ?

According to legend, the first Indian puppeteer or Nat was brought to life by the Creator Brahma to entertain his wife, Saraswati. Saraswati was so pleased to watch the puppets perform that the puppeteer was sent to earth.

Pottery

Pottery making is one of the oldest crafts. The blue tile used in pottery originated in Egypt. It finally reached India where it came to be known as 'Delhi Blue' as it was used in the monuments and buildings in Delhi. The traditional Persian Pottery designs evolved and adapted into more sophisticated ones. From pots and vases, the products have become increasingly innovative.

Puppetry

The Kathputali community is a group of nomadic artists who settled in Delhi in 1950. They are among the world's largest community of puppeteers and street performers.

Ittar Making

Ittars are perfumes made of fresh flowers and oils. Delhi's oldest perfumery is Gulab Singh Johri Mal in Old Delhi. It is believed that the original owner of the shop used to showcase his Ittars in the court of Akbar Shah II (1806-1837).

Calligraphy

Calligraphy is the art of decorative handwriting or lettering. Establishment of the Delhi Sultanate saw the introduction of calligraphy in India. The 12th century witnessed the use of calligraphy on buildings, arms, art objects, as we see in the beautiful inscriptions that adorn the Qutub Minar. During the Mughal Period, calligraphy reached its peak.

MY PUPPET EXPERIENCE!

Recount your first experience of watching a puppet show. Describe the first puppet you made. How old were you then?

Paper Craft

Tazia is a popular Paper Craft of Delhi. These are commemorative, intricately-cut paper pasted on a bamboo frame used during Muharram processions. The Tazia makers also make them from flowers for the annual Phoolwalon-ki-Sair. We can also see fabulous paper kites adorning the sky during Independence Day.

Zardozi

Zardozi is an elaborate style of metal embroidery. It is derived from two Persian words 'zar' meaning gold and 'dos' meaning embroidery or work. Zari work was an ancient art form used to decorate and design the royal garments and other royal items like pillow covers, bed sheets and so on. Initially, embroidery was done using silver wires and real gold leaves.

Jewellery

Jewellery makers or Saadegars are craftsmen skilled in the art of setting navratna or nine precious stones in gold. They settled in Delhi during the reign of Shahjahan. Dariba Kalan in Chandni Chowk is famous for its jewellery.

MY FAVOURITE CRAFT TRADITION

Select a craft tradition that interests you. Locate a craftsperson skilled in that particular craft and interview them. Some questions you may ask:

- How long have they been practicing the craft?
- How did they learn?
- How old were they when they started training?
- Who taught them?
- Would they like their children to learn it too?
- Stories or legends associated with the craft.

After interviewing the craftsperson, research and find out more about the craft, how it evolved over the ages and how it has been accepted in society.

Make a scrapbook of your findings.

DID YOU KNOW ?

The Rashtrapati Bhavan Museum is unique as it houses gifts received by the Presidents, rare photographs, heritage furniture, the president's study and more. It is set up in the earlier Clock Tower, stables, and garage.

Centres for Crafts

Ayyanar Terracotta Horse, Anandagram

Dilli Haat is a vibrant craft bazaar selling handicrafts. It is located at INA, Janak Puri, and Pitampura. Here, stalls are allotted to craftsmen to showcase their products from all over India over a fortnight.

The Delhi Cottage Emporium of the government works towards preserving and nurturing the work of skilled artisans and protecting India's rich heritage. Delhi also best showcases the crafts of our states in the diverse State Emporiums.

National Crafts Museum and Sanskriti Foundation (Anandagram) contributes towards promoting traditional crafts and cultures as well.

Museums and Galleries

Seal, Harappan Civilization, National Museum

Bride's Toilet by Amrita Sher-Gil, National Gallery of Modern Art

- **National Museum** is one of the largest museums in India. It houses around three lakh articles ranging from the Pre-Historic to the Modern Period.
- **National Gallery of Modern Art** is one of the largest modern art museums in the world. It houses paintings by artists such as Amrita Sher-Gil, Abanindranath Tagore, Jamini Roy, Raja Ravi Varma among others.
- **National Gandhi Museum** houses artifacts associated with the life of Mahatma Gandhi, such as relics, memorabilia, books, journals, documents and photographs.
- **Indira Gandhi National Centre for the Arts** is a centre for studying and experiencing the plethora of arts from across the country.
- **Rabindra Bhavan** constituted by the Lalit Kala Akademi, Sangeet Natak Akademi, Sahitya Akademi, is another institution dedicated to promoting the arts – music, dance, fine arts, and literature.
- **National Rail Museum** displays electric, steam, diesel locomotives, exquisite royal saloons, and artifacts. It captures 163 years of the Indian railway history.
- **The Nehru Memorial Museum** was the residence of the British Commander-in-Chief of the Indian Army, later the home of India's first Prime Minister, Jawaharlal Nehru. It preserves and showcases the history of our independence monument.

FUN WITH ART

Miniature paintings are so detailed that we can learn much about the customs of that time through them.

Create your own miniature painting:

Create your own miniature painting illustrating a regular day in your home or an important festival.

Material:

A4 white drawing paper, pencils, paints, variety of small to medium paint brushes, gold markers, a miniature painting sample.

Method:

- Mark a quarter-inch border around the edge of the drawing paper.
- Cover the piece of paper with paint as background and let it dry. This will be used to demonstrate the process of applying wet paint over dried paint. For example, it is simpler to paint the whole sky blue and then dab on the stars, than paint the stars and try to go around each one with the blue paint.
- Draw outlines of the figures you want to paint with a pencil. Do not give it any detailing.
- After drawing, paint these figures with a base colour and let it dry.
- Once the painting has dried, use a variety of small brushes to fill the figures and background with details and patterns.
- Draw a pattern on the margin of the paper to create a frame around the painting. You could use gold markers to give it a royal look.

Colour the given painting:

Colour the given painting outline and fill it with intricate detailing creatively in the Mughal miniature style.

COMMUNITY AND YOU

The society in Delhi has seen a harmonious mixture of people from all over the country. Many diverse cultures and ethnic groups can be found here. Different localities in this culturally rich city are famous for their association with different communities, such as Majnu ka Tila, Chittranjan Park, Punjabi Bagh etc. Over the years, there has been an expansion of language and dialects in Delhi, sometimes along with an amalgamation as well. The dialect is known as Khariboli. It truly reflects the diversity of Delhi. During the Medieval Period, many Urdu poets, such as Zauk, hailed from Delhi.

Delhi is a truly cosmopolitan city, with an identity so varied that everyone who stays here feels at home. There are people practising many different religions here. Delhi is home to a Parsi Anjuman (Parsi Association), which has a rest house, fire temple dedicated to the Parsi God, Zarathushtra, and a cemetery.

We can see the unity in diversity well in the intangible heritage of this city where all cultures get represented and celebrated with equal enthusiasm. The excitement with which Diwali is celebrated is matched by the Durga Puja festivities. Christmas decorations light up the city, while the mosques and dargahs prepare for Eid.

Delhi has many places of worship. According to the 2011 census, Delhi's population includes Hindus, Muslims, Christians, Sikhs, Parsis, Buddhists, and Jews.

DID YOU KNOW?

The language which evolved and developed around Delhi is popularly known as Zaban-e-Dehli or 'the language of Delhi'. It inspired a number of poets in the Medieval period.

TRYST WITH TRADITION

All communities have traditional customs and beliefs that they follow for important life events such as weddings, births, etc. Choose a community and find out about all the rituals they perform at any one such event. Find out the following details about them:

- Which event are they performed for?
- Who performs the ritual?
- What is the significance behind the ritual?
- Does it have a scientific reasoning? If so, what is it?

Hanuman Temple

Temples

Chattarpur Temple, the second largest temple complex in India is dedicated to Goddess Katyayani. It was established in 1974, by Baba Sant Nagpal. The temple complex is made from marble.

ISKON Temple is dedicated to Radha and Krishna and was setup as a centre for Vedic knowledge. Built with red stone and marble, it is well-known for its unique design.

Hanuman Temple at Connaught Place is an ancient Hindu temple and is said to be one of the five temples from the Mahabharata days.

Gurudwaras

Gurudwara Bangla Sahib is associated with Guru Har Krishan, the eighth Sikh guru. It was built in 1783, under the reign of Shaḥ Alam II, a member of Aurangzeb's darbar. Earlier, this place was the bungalow (or bangla) of Raja Jai Singh and was called Jaisinghpura Palace. It is because of this that it is today known as 'Bangla' Sahib.

Gurudwara Sis Ganj Sahib is one of the nine historical Gurudwaras in Delhi and is located in Chandni Chowk. It was built to commemorate the death of Guru Tegh Bahadur. The gurudwara marks the site where the Guru was beheaded on the orders of the Mughal Emperor Aurangzeb for refusing to convert to Islam.

Jain Temples

Digambar Jain Temple is the oldest Jain temple in Delhi. It was built by the Agarwal Jain community under the reign of Emperor Shah Jahan, south of Chandni Chowk in Old Delhi. The second building behind the temple is the Jain Bird Hospital.

DID YOU KNOW ?

It is believed that the crescent moon on top of the finial of Hanuman Temple was given to the temple by one of the Mughal Emperors.

Gurudwara Bangla Sahib

CARE FOR COMMUNITY

Like Gurudwaras organise langars and Jains have the Bird Hospital, all religious communities work towards the collective upliftment of the society. Select any one religious community and discuss the ways in which they contribute to the betterment of the people.

Sacred Heart Cathedral

Jama Masjid

Churches

Located near Kashmiri Gate, The St. James' Church is among the oldest churches of Delhi. It was built by Colonel James Skinner, an Anglo-Indian military adventurer in India, in 1836. Thomas Metcalfe was buried here.

Cathedral Church of the Redemption is also known as the Viceroy Church. It was used by the British Viceroy. Located near the Rashtrapati Bhavan, it is built of red sandstone and Burmese teak and was opened in 1931. The design is inspired by the 16th century church of II Redentore in Venice.

Mosques

Jama Masjid is the largest mosque in India. Situated near the Red Fort in Delhi, it is one of the last monuments built by the Mughal Emperor Shah Jahan. It has a splendid peripheral and a fine-looking interior made with marble. It took six years to complete this monument.

Fatehpuri Masjid was built in 1650 by Fatehpuri Begum, one of Shah Jahan's wives. The mosque was built using red sandstone and has a fluted dome. Flanked by minarets, the mosque has a traditional design with the prayer hall having seven-arched openings.

Dargahs

Hazrat Nizamuddin Auliya's Dagah is located in the Nizamuddin area. Close to it stands a baoli which was built to ensure a steady water supply for pilgrims and villagers. Today, at the Dargah, qawwalis are sung for the saint every Thursday.

Chiragh-i-Delhi Dargah is situated in the village of Chiragh Delhi. In this dargah, the disciple of Nizammudin Auliya, Nasiruddin Chiragh Dehlavi is buried. He was also referred to as *Roshan Chiragh e Dehlvi* (the Illuminated Lamp of Delhi).

LESSER KNOWN COMMUNITIES

Find out about any lesser known religious communities found in India. Find out the following details –

- Name of religion.
- Monotheistic or Polytheistic.
- How old is the religion?
- Do they believe in idol worship?
- What percentage of the population follows this?
- Describe any one of their rituals.

DID YOU KNOW ?

Delhi has one Jewish synogogue, called Judah Hyam Synogogue along with a cemetery, near Khan Market and one Parsi Fire Temple or Dar-e Mehr on Bahadur Shah Zafar Marg.

COLOURFUL FESTIVALS

Eid

Eid al-Fitr is the festival of breaking the fast. It is celebrated at the end of the month of Ramadan, which is the holy month of fasting from dawn to sunset. Sawaiyan or sweetened vermicelli is prepared and enjoyed by all.

Navaratri

This nine-day festival is met with great enthusiasm. In the north Indian celebrations, this constitutes of Ramlila, culminating in the Dussehra festival by burning Ravana effigies. In the Bengali community, the festivities involve many pandals, with beautiful idols of Goddess Durga on a decorated stage.

Diwali

This festival marks the return of Lord Rama to Ayodhya after his fourteen years of exile. In the days approaching Diwali, melas are set up and plays and skits are performed depicted the story of Ramayana.

Chhath

It is a four-day long festival dedicated to the worship of the Sun God and his wife, Usha, thanking them for bestowing life on earth and granting wishes. The festival includes rigorous practices like holy bathing, fasting, offering to the rising Sun.

Christmas

This festival commemorates the birth of Jesus Christ. Market areas are decorated with lights and Christmas decoration and Christmas carols are sung in churches, along with the Mass.

Other than these festivals, there are many other that are celebrated with equal amount of fervour in the capital. Some of these festivals are, Holi, Baisakhi, Lohri, Onam, Pongal, and many more!

Festival of Harmony: Phoolwalon ki Sair

Phoolwalon ki Sair, meaning the procession of florists, has become a symbol of communal harmony and national integration. During this festival, people of different communities come together to offer chaadar and pankha at the Dargah of Hazrat Qutbuddin Bakhtiyar Kaki and Devi Yogmaya Temple.

SHARED COLOURS

Have you ever participated in a festival or celebration of another community or religion? Describe the rituals, the traditional food items, the similarities and differences with a similar occasion in your community.

CAPITAL CELEBRATES

WORDS OF WISDOM

"If we are to reach real peace in this world, we should start with children".

Above is a well-known quote on peace by Mahatma Gandhi. Why do you think he said this? Interpret the quote and write how it is relevant in today's world.

PEACEFUL TIES

Using interesting braiding techniques make a peace or a friendship band with recycled material.

India has three officially declared national holidays –

Republic Day

Republic Day commemorates the Indian constitution coming into force on January 26th, 1950. The Delhi Republic Day Parade is the largest and most important parade that marks the Republic Day celebrations. It takes place every year at Rajpath. The ceremony is started by the hoisting of the Indian flag by the President, following which the Parade commences. Every year on Republic Day, India invites a head of state, who is the chief guest for the ceremony.

The Beating Retreat ceremony marks the end of the Republic Day Celebrations. It takes place on the 29th of January. It is performed by bands of the three wings of the Indian military: the Army, Navy, and Air Force.

Independence Day

Independence Day takes place annually to commemorate India's independence from the British on 15th August 1947. The celebration includes the President's address on the eve of Independence Day, followed by the unfurling of the Indian flag at the Red Fort by the Prime Minister the next day, and a speech discussing the achievements of the past year and the heroic deeds of those who fought for our independence. A march past takes places and finally the national anthem is sung.

Gandhi Jayanti

Gandhi Jayanti is celebrated every year on the event of Mahatma Gandhi's birthday. Internationally, this day is marked as International Day of Non-Violence due to his strong principles of ahimsa or non-violence. In India, it is marked by prayer services and tributes in all states. People visit Raj Ghat, which is a memorial dedicated to Gandhi ji, to pay tribute to him.

Red Fort

FOOD FUSION

Food has been a very important part of Delhi's culture. **Old Delhi**, in its crammed alleyways has preserved this aspect of our city's heritage very well. Till date, one will find street vendors selling delicious, tempting chaats and other food items at every corner. Food for us is so important that a street in Old Delhi has actually been named after a food item – Paranthe wali Gali, because of the variety of stuffed paranthe that are available there.

It seems like Delhi has absorbed the food habits of all those who invaded or migrated to Delhi and adapted these habits to favour the taste buds of its residents. The Mughals introduced exotic fruits and the cooking of food in ghee with a helping of dry fruits. The British brought to India the potato, which is now the mainstay of Delhi street food in its aloo chaats, kulchas etc. Bania food can also be seen being cooked and consumed by the public in Old Delhi. The Punjabis got the tandoor and tikka which are enjoyed by all. The present day Mughlai food is a mixture of Punjabi and the actual Mughal cuisine.

Some famous street food items from Delhi are – Daulat ki chaat, golgappas, shakarkandi, shahi tukra, rabri faluda, kulfi, jalebi, phirni etc. most of which can still be found being relished in Old Delhi. South Extension is known for its famous bhel puri and Bengali Market for its golgappas.

From incorporating foods from our invaders, we have now reached a time when the landscape of street food is changing to include foods even from our neighbouring countries. Today, every corner can be seen with a stall selling delicious momos. These dumplings have actually originated from Tibet and are today being enjoyed in the city of Delhi. It is developments like this that show us how inclusive and assimilative Delhi is capable of being.

DID YOU KNOW ?

Nahari is one of the famous dishes from Chandni Chowk. There was a nehar (small canal or rivulet) in Chandni Chowk, with stagnant water, which got people sick. The hakims urged the people to eat nahari. The protein and spices cured them.

SUMMER COOLERS

Traditional summer coolers have interesting stories behind them. Hakeem Majeed – a Yunani physician – launched Rooh Afza from his clinic in Old Delhi in 1907.

- Find out stories and legends associated with other such traditional summer coolers.

FOOD FIESTA

Like Delhi, each city has specific food items that they are famous for.

- Jot down a few of your favourite dishes from your own city and the place where they have originated from.
- Write down the ingredients and recipes of these dishes and try making them at home!

Daulat ki chaat

LITERARY ICONS

Writings of the Royals!

Mughal Emperors used to get biographies written for them. Shah Jahan was one such ruler whose biography known as Padshahnama was written by Abdul Hamid Lahori. This enthusiasm for writing continued till the last emperor, Bahadur Shah Zafar, who himself was a poet. He appointed Ghalib as the poet tutor as well as the royal historian at the court.

LANGUAGE THEN AND NOW

Talk to your grandparents and find out about an old dialect popularly spoken in your state. Write some common sentences in that dialect and their translation in the language that is spoken today.

Over the years, Delhi has acquired an interesting literary identity. Delhi has evolved its own accepted language, Khariboli, which became the base language in North India. With this development in language, there was an increased interest in literature, making Delhi fertile for many writers and poets.

Ancient

In the Ancient Period, writing was mostly used for proclamations by rulers in inscriptions that laid out rules and regulations. Delhi had however been mentioned in other texts. Hindu texts mention Delhi with its Sanskrit name Hasthinapur, meaning elephant-city. According to legends, Indraprastha of the Mahabharata was perhaps, Delhi. In some Buddhist texts, Indapatta is described as the capital of the Kuru Kingdom.

Medieval

In the Medieval Period, writing and documenting became a very important art as rulers wanted their achievements written and remembered forever. Thus, they patronised many writers and poets and encouraged their works.

Amir Khusrau was a poet, scholar, and musician in the Delhi Sultanate. He wrote in Persian and Hindavi. Abu'l-Fazl ibn Mubarak was the author of the official history of Akbar's reign – Akbarnama, while his brother, Faizi was the Emperor's poet laureate.

Modern

In the Modern Period, writing began to be used as a medium to voice opinions. Authors took their writings as a platform to discuss the nation's freedom. Pandit Jawaharlal Nehru wrote about the freedom struggle in his book 'Toward Freedom'. Some other well-known Modern Period writers are Kamla Bhasin, Khushwant Singh, Raghuvir Sahay, Nirmal Verma, Urvashi Butalia, Arundhati Roy, Manju Kapur and many more.

Delhi has also been an attractive subject for writers and scholars from around the world, such as Percival Spear, R. V. Smith, and William Dalrymple.

MY CITY TODAY

The city of Delhi has changed enormously. This can be seen in the way the architecture has changed from the medieval forts and palaces to today's concrete high-rise buildings. Living in Delhi, one cannot help but be amazed at all the culture and history at every corner while we still continuously embrace new lifestyles. Let's look at the organizations that make sure that we can live a life like this – modern, yet surrounded by history!

Managing Delhi Today

Enormous efforts are required to keep our city, its parks and streets, clean. The city is managed by the following organizations:

The **Municipal Corporation of Delhi (MCD)** is responsible for all the civic amenities like water, building construction, roads, among other activities.

NDMC
नई दिल्ली नगरपालिका परिषद्

The **New Delhi Municipal Council (NDMC)** can be traced to the Imperial Delhi Committee which was created in 1913 to overlook the construction of the new capital. The NDMC consists of 28 departments which include Public Health, Welfare, Electricity etc.

The **Delhi Development Authority (DDA)** oversees the development of new residential extension areas.

The **Delhi Jal Board**, **Delhi Metro Rail Corporation (DMRC)**, **Public Works Department (PWD)** etc. are some of the other agencies which look after the city.

Delhi Metro – Artsy Craftsy!

The Delhi Metro has emerged as a major pulsating lifeline of the city. Some stations show their love for heritage, such as at INA station through the displays of traditional textiles. At Jor Bagh and Green Park metro stations, DMRC and INTACH have created a photo-exhibition depicting the historical monuments present around the Jor Bagh area. A Heritage Line has also been inaugurated, which has four stations – Delhi Gate, Kashmiri Gate, Jama Masjid, and Red Fort. INTACH is actively involved in art installations along this Heritage Line.

- Can you find out the monument signages developed by INTACH displayed at some of the metro stations?

PLAN OF ACTION

As a first step, a responsible citizen can:

- Visit any site or monument.
- Take photos and videos documenting its heritage.
- Bring it to the attention of the concerned authorities.
- Make a report of any tree-cutting, waste disposal, poaching, or similar activities which threaten the heritage.
- Find out whether the heritage site is included in any form of listing or notified under any regulations.
- Create a street play to spread awareness about that heritage site and why it should be protected.

TAKING CARE OF YOUR CITY

As the youth, it is your responsibility to care of your city.

- Think about what you can do to improve your city and make a list of good citizen resolutions for yourself – 'I will' or 'will not'.

  For example: I will not litter. I will save water.
- Now brainstorm a project to implement these resolutions in your neighbourhood, school, or home.
- Draw up an action plan with steps and deadlines:

  Aim:

  Planning:

  Execution:

  Phase 1:

  Phase 2:

  Phase 3:

  Evaluation:

Being citizens of India,
take up heritage issues
as your personal responsibility.

BIBLIOGRAPHY

Books

Natural Heritage

Dhawale, Meenakshi. *Narratives Of The Environment Of Delhi' A Ramble In The Archives And Reminiscences.* INTACH Natural Heritage Division, 2010.

Exploring a tree: Teachers Manual by Centre for Environment Education and Nehru Foundation for Development.

Help Delhi Breathe : A guide to your role in saving Delhi's Environment by Youth Reach.

Identification Manual For Indian Wildlife, Species And Derivatives In Trade. Eds. Malik and Menon, WWF-India (Prepared by TRAFFICIndia), 1996.

Krishna, Nanditha. *Sacred Animals Of India.* Penguin Books India, 2010.

Krishen, Pradeep. *Trees Of Delhi: A Field Guide.* Dorling Kindersley (India) Pvt. Limited, 2006.

Knowledge, Attitude And Practises Of Delhiites Towards The River Yamuna. A Report by Peace Institute Charitable Trust and CMS Environment, 2009.

Lal, Ranjit. *Birds From My Window.* Tulika, 2002.

Master Plan For Delhi With The Perspective For The Year 2021. New Delhi: Rupa & Co., 2007.

Naturalising Delhi: A Plan for Enhancing Climate Resilience, Urban Biodiversity and Habitats, Natural Heritage Division, INTACH New Delhi, 2015.

Singh, Samar, *Birds of IIC*, India International Centre, 2007.

Smetacek, Peter. *The Butterflies Of Delhi.* Kalpavriksh, Environment Action Group, 2000.

The Delhi Ridge Forest: Decline And Conservation. Kalpavriksh, 1991.

WWF-India, Can the Clock be Turned Back? Delhi Environment Status Report (New Delhi: Pollution Monitoring & Technology Co-operation Division), WWF-India, 1996.

Zaidi, Mehran. *Birds and Butterflies of Delhi.* Tara Press, 2010.

Built Heritage

Alkazi, Feisal and Jain, Priti. *Exploring The River Front of My Town.* Centre for Environment Education, Ahmedabad.

Ali, Salim. *The Book of Indian Birds*, eleventh edition. Publication of the Bombay Natural History Society Oxford University Press 1992.

Gupta, Narayani and Masselos, Jim. *Beato's Delhi 1857, 1997.* Ravi Dayal Publisher, 2000.

Gupta, Narayani, *Let's Explore Humayun's Tomb.* The Archaeological Survey of India in collaboration with Aga Khan Trust for Culture, 2011.

Jain, A.K. *The Cities of Delhi.* Management Publishing Co. 1994.

Jain, A. K. *Dillinama: The Cities Of Delhi.* Synergy Books India, 2013.

Peck, Lucy. *Delhi, A Thousand Years Of Building.* The Lotus Collection, 2006.

Punja, Shobita, and Rohini Kandhari. *A Capital Story – The Building Of New Delhi (1911-1931).* Indian National Trust for Art and Cultural Heritage (INTACH), Heritage Education and Communication Service (HECS), 2003.

Smith, R. V. *The Delhi That No-One Knows.* Chronicle Books, an imprint of DC Publishers, 2005.

Spear, Percival, Narayani Gupta, and Laura Sykes. *Delhi: Its Monuments And History.* 3rd ed. Oxford India Paperbacks, 2008.

Singh, B. P. and Verma, Pavan K. *The Millennium Book on New Delhi*, Oxford University Press, 2001.

INTACH Delhi Chapter, *The Red Fort and its Surroundings.*

Living Heritage

Dayal, Mala. *Celebrating Delhi.* Ravi Dayal Publisher, 2010.

Krishna Menon, A.G, Swapna Liddle, and Annabel Lopez.
Delhi: A Living Heritage. IGNCA and INTACH, 2010.

Peck, Lucy. *Delhi, A Thousand Years Of Building.* The Lotus Collection, 2006.

Spear, Percival, Narayani Gupta and Laura Sykes. *Delhi: Its Monuments And History.* 3rd ed. Oxford India Paperbacks, 2008.

Online References

Natural Heritage

http://indianexpress.com/article/cities/delhi/aravalli-range-hillsmangar-bani-this-is-whats-left-of-a-forest-ecosystem-environmentwildlife-human-habitation-4901951/.

http://www.thehindu.com/news/cities/Delhi/butterfly-park-opensto-public/

http://timesofindia.indiatimes.com/city/delhi/ncrcomes- out-for-its-first-butterfly-count/

http://www.thehindu.com/todays-paper/tp-national/tp-newdelhi/ on-a-wing-at-lodhi-garden-butterfly-conservatory/

http://www.scholarpedia.org/article/Butterfly_effect

http://delhigreens.com/2017/06/04/tughlaqabad-biodiversity-parkcelebrate-first-environment-day/.

https://www.sahapedia.org/yamuna-biodiversity-park-overview

Built Heritage

http://www.akdn.org/news/humayuns-tomb-conservation-completed

https://www.google.com/culturalinstitute/beta/exhibit/QRUUiMQd

https://olddelhiheritage.in/darya-ganj-bazar/

http://www.havelidharampura.com/restoration-of-haveli/

https://www.delhiinformation.in/tourism/tombstombswithinhumayun tombcomplex.html

https://rangandatta.wordpress.com/2017/05/10/baolis-step-wells-ofdelhi/

https://dillikadarshan.wordpress.com/where-all/humayuns-tomb complex/matka-pirs-dargah/

http://www.monumentsofdelhi.com/cities

http://delhi-timeline.in/

http://whc.unesco.org/en/tentativelists/5743/

Living Heritage

http://akshardham.com/explore/water-show/

http://www.delhimetrorail.com

https://www.metmuseum.org/toah/hd/cpin/hd_cpin.htm

https://selfstudyhistory.com/2015/01/27/mughal-music/

http://www.hindustantimes.com/art-and-culture/crafted-in-clay-the-artof-pottery-in-delhi

http://spicmacay.com/

http://indianexpress.com/article/lifestyle/books/the-life-andpoetry-ofbahadurshah-zafar-remembering-the-last-mughal-emperorand-hispoetry4681256/

Heritage Education and Communication Service (HECS)

The Indian National Trust for Art and Cultural Heritage (INTACH) is India's largest non-profit membership organization dedicated to conservation and preservation of India's natural, cultural, living, tangible and intangible heritage.

Recognizing the importance of heritage education in spreading awareness among the people, INTACH set up the Heritage Education and Communication Service (HECS) in 1998. Since its inception, HECS is working to create awareness among different target groups such as, the public, professionals, city and local authorities, INTACH chapters, school and college teachers, and students. It designs different types of training programmes to make citizens aware of their role in the conservation and preservation of their natural, cultural and living heritage.

HECS Educational Projects

HECS has developed several innovative programmes and modules in heritage education for school children using radio, television, film and internet.

National Teacher Training Workshops on Heritage Awareness

The HECS team in collaboration with INTACH Chapter Convenors and with the funding from the Government of India conducts workshops on heritage awareness for teachers in different parts of the country. Till date, over 185 workshops have been conducted successfully.

Join Our Heritage Club Network for Schools

Become a Member of INTACH

Help Conserve India's Heritage

College Heritage Volunteer Training Programme

A pioneering initiative that aims at sensitizing undergraduate college students to protect their heritage and train them to lead a nation-wide movement for heritage conservation and preservation. Since its launch in 2012, over 20 workshops and five forums have been organized.

Heritage Clubs

The Heritage Clubs in schools are designed to create awareness and inspire students to participate in heritage-related activities in school and in their locality. HECS has a nation-wide network of heritage clubs in around 3900 schools across cities and towns in the country.

JAGO – Heritage and Citizenship

Presents ways of becoming more informed and active citizens through engagement with heritage by exploring inter-linkages between heritage and citizenship for enthusiastic citizens.

National Outreach Programmes

Our national programmes, like India Heritage Quiz, Clean Monument National Campaign, FilmIt India help nurture cultural understanding, care and concern amongst school children about India's unique and diverse heritage.

Some HECS Publications

Hands on Heritage: A handbook with over 100 activities, work-sheets and innovative ideas on learning about India's rich cultural and natural heritage.

A Capital Story: A small booklet on the making of the New Delhi, its architects, how the site was chosen, the design and architectural features of Rashtrapati Bhavan and other buildings in the vicinity.

Adopt A Monument: A handbook for teachers, students and enthusiasts who want to learn how to conserve India's magnificent built heritage.

Adopt A Tree: A handbook for teachers, students, and enthusiasts committed to conserve our natural heritage.

Adopt A Craft: A handbook for teachers, students and enthusiasts who want to explore the different crafts practiced in India. It explains in detail the various methods for learning and caring for crafts.

Care For Heritage: A handbook for teachers, students and enthusiasts explains steps for restoration and conservation of art objects or artefacts.

JAGO: Heritage and Citizenship: Presents ways of becoming more active and informed citizens through constructive civic engagement with heritage and support good citizenship initiatives.

The Hornbill Warrior – Know Nagaland (A Colouring Book): The storybook-cum-colouring book brings out the heritage of Nagaland as discovered through the eyes of a young Naga girl.

India Unlimited... My Travel Diary: The publication explores India's diverse heritage, covering all of its states and union territories. In this journal, one can record one's travel and cultural and heritage experiences.

Off We Go! Series: These storybooks follow three children visiting the cities of Delhi, Kolkata, and Mumbai during their holidays. While they travel around the cities, they explore the various facets of their heritage.

About **INTACH**

The Indian National Trust for Art and Cultural Heritage (INTACH) is India's largest non-profit membership-based organization dedicated to conservation and preservation of India's natural, cultural, living, tangible, and intangible heritage. Its mission is to:

- Sensitize the public about the pluralistic cultural legacy of India;
- Instill a sense of social responsibility towards preserving our common heritage;
- Protect and conserve our living, built, and natural heritage by undertaking necessary actions and measures;
- Document unprotected buildings of archaeological, architectural, historical and aesthetic significance; and cultural resources, as this is the first step towards formulating conservation plans;
- Develop heritage policy and regulations, and make legal interventions to protect our heritage when necessary;
- Provide expertise in the field of conservation, restoration and preservation of specific works of art; and encourage capacity building by developing skills through training programmes;
- Undertake emergency response measures during natural or man-made disasters, and support local administration whenever heritage is threatened;
- Foster collaborations, Memoranda of Understanding (MoUs) and partnerships with government and other national and international agencies; and
- Generate sponsorships for conservation and educational projects.

talking CUB

About **Talking Cub**

Talking Cub is the children's imprint of Speaking Tiger Books. Launched in December 2017, the imprint has published over fifty books, including those by renowned authors such as Ruskin Bond, Paro Anand, Ranjit Lal, Subhadra Sen Gupta, Deepa Agarwal and others. Some of the country's best fiction and non-fiction writing for children is part of the imprint. The details of all the titles can be seen at www.speakingtigerbooks.com